DR WILLIAM KITCHINER
REGENCY ECCENTRIC

Other titles published in the Southover Historic Cookery and Housekeeping Series:

William Verrall's Cookery Book
First published in 1759, with an Introduction by Colin Brent

The London Art of Cookery
By John Farley. First published in 1783, with an Introduction by Stephen Medcalf

The Complete Servant
By Samuel and Sarah Adams. First published in 1825, with an Introduction by Pamela Horn

The English Bread Book
By Eliza Acton. First published in 1859, with an Introduction by Elizabeth Ray

Alexis Soyer: Cook Extraordinary
By Elizabeth Ray, with an Introduction by Prue Leith

Series Editor, Ann Haly

To all Great British Eccentrics

DR WILLIAM KITCHINER

REGENCY ECCENTRIC

Author of The Cook's Oracle

BY

TOM BRIDGE

&

COLIN COOPER ENGLISH

Southover Press
1992

First published 1992 by
SOUTHOVER PRESS
2 Cockshut Road, Lewes, East Sussex BN7 1JH
Copyright © Tom Bridge
© Colin Cooper English
ISBN 1-870962-07-9
Phototypeset in Berling 10.5/12.5 by Screenset, Seaford
Printed in England on antique wove wood-free paper by
Villiers Publications Ltd, 26A Shepherds Hill, London N6 5AH
for Southover Press

British Library Cataloguing-in-Publication Data.
A catalogue record for this book is available from the
British Library

CONTENTS

FOREWORD

During my many years of research into British culinary and kitchen history, I have often come across the name of William Kitchiner. But such references have never been very extensive or explicit – usually just a passing mention of his best known book, *The Cook's Oracle*, or, sometimes, one of his more *outré* recipes, such as wow-wow sauce or spatchcocked eels.

Florence White, the doyenne of English folk cookery, quotes several of his recipes in *Good Things in England* (1932) and so does Elizabeth Ayrton in the more recent *The Cookery of England* (1974). But otherwise William Kitchiner has been curiously overlooked by most modern cookery writers.

A cursory allusion to him as the 'celebrated doctor' in a chef's manual of the early 1890's suggests that his name was a household word among Victorian cooks and gourmets. If that is so, it has certainly suffered an eclipse during the present century and has now sunk into obscurity along with the books he wrote and the songs he sang to welcome his nightly guests to his house in Fitzroy Square.

But now Tom Bridge and Colin Cooper English have succeeded in revealing Kitchiner as a many-sided and fascinating character; a complex mixture of egotist, bonvivant, eccentric, pedagogue, man about town, charlatan and imposter.

The authors are professional caterers, so their research has naturally centred on Kitchiner's culinary interests and especially on his book, *The Cook's Oracle*, which, published privately in 1817, rapidly established itself in the market and influenced the style and pattern of subsequent cookery books, including those by Eliza Acton and Mrs Isabella Beeton. It is to their credit that they have unpeeled the onion layers of so unpredictable an individual.

It is a pity that there are few records of the fate of Kitchiner's bastard son. His disappearance from the Victorian scene suggests that he may have speedily squandered the fortune he acquired from his father's early death in 1827. If so, it was another example of the Lancashire dictum: 'Clogs to clogs in three generations'.

Reg Baker

Late Editorial Consultant to the Caterer and Hotel Keeper, who died in 1991.

Acknowledgements

When we started writing this book, we had no idea of the amount of research it would take to complete our task. Without the willing co-operation of many patient people, historians, archivists, librarians, publishers, curators and specialists, our work would have been incomplete.

We would like to thank the Bolton historian, William D Billington, for his work deciphering Dr William Kitchiner's 1826 Will for us, and Dr Patrick Moore, CBE, FRAS, for his great help in unravelling Dr Kitchiner's interest in optics and telescopes. Eric Quayle's wonderful collection of books proved immensely useful, also his very rare Kitchiner memorabilia.

We are likewise indebted to the following for all their help: the staff of the Bolton Reference Library; the staff of Kendal Public Library; Neil Foster; Duncan McAra; Sandy Collinson; Alwynne Wheeler and Solene Morris of the Department of Zoology at the British Museum (Natural History); The Meat Promotion Executive; the staff at the British Library Reading Room; The British Museum (Prints and Drawings); the B.B.C. Music Library and the British Library Music Library; The Times Newspaper Library; The Hulton Picture Library, and The Guildhall Library (Prints and Maps), Aldermanbury, London.

We would like to thank the bursar and archivist at St. John's College, Cambridge; Mrs Mary Cockram of Brookwood Cemetery, Woking, Surrey; Miss M.J.Swarbrick and John Sargent, archivists at the City of Westminster Public Library, London; Major Mike Chignell of the Recorder's Office at Charterhouse School, Godalming, Surrey; Chris Nottage, verger of St. Pancras Parish Church, and Ann Bagnall for her confidence in our work.

HOW WE BECAME INTERESTED

IN

DR KITCHINER

What really fired our enthusiasm was an old volume we found lying on the shelves of a secondhand bookshop in London. This was *The Cook's Oracle* (1817) by William Kitchiner, MD, or Dr Kitchiner as he was better known. Our edition was 1827. When we started reading it we realised that here was the most extraordinary, the most entertaining and the most bizarre cookery book of the nineteenth century. There is even a chapter on culinary curiosities from an earlier and more primitive age, which gave a rare look at strange dishes such as pies made from live birds, lizards in hot broth, and a cat in jelly among others. There has never been another cookery book quite like it and, not surprisingly, it became a best seller.

Reading through its fascinating recipes and accounts of day-to-day Regency life we came to a section on spit-roasting. This description of the process, clear, exciting and persuasive, was so impressive that we decided to put William Kitchiner's procedure to the test by building our own roasting spit according to his nineteenth century principles, and see if we could recapture the taste of true spit-roasted meat.

In 1986 we started designing our machine. It had to be capable of being transported from site to site, be easily assembled before work and taken down afterwards. It had to be big, enclosed in its own framework, to be covered with a canopy, and have a carving section. To comply with modern Environmental Health regulations, it also had to have a portable wash handbasin with hot running water. We designed that as well.

By early 1987 our machine was built. It was capable of cooking two sheep or two pigs or two hundredweight of meat at once on two spits.

It was used at a Country and Western Music Festival and also used at the opening ceremony of a new Theme Park in the North, which has since become famous. It went out to Guy Fawkes night celebrations, and was used at a water skiing gala, and at records week on Lake Windermere, when international power boat racers gather for one week each October to make their attempts to break water speed record.

This was about as close as we could get to true spit-roasted meat. Being roasted in the open air it is not cooked in a moist atmosphere, so has a dry succulent taste, and is utterly delicious.

Old cookery books are among the richest sources of social and economic history that are available. Our reading of them has made it clear to us that cookery, like life, is constantly evolving.

The secret of Dr Kitchiner's success was meticulous attention to detail. He was not himself a cook, but before he embarked on *The Cook's Oracle* he read every cookery book he could find, which amounted to some two hundred and fifty volumes. While writing his book, he taught himself to cook, claiming that every single recipe in *The Cook's Oracle* had been prepared and served to his *Committee of Taste* for approval before being committed to print.

Many of the terms Kitchiner uses may seem strange and unfamiliar now. For instance, he describes "frothing" his roasts before the spit, and "crimping" his salmon. He recommends using a gridiron or cooking in a Dutch oven, and describes stewpans rather than saucepans. Wherever he uses such terms we have added our own explanation, and there is also a small glossary at the end of the book. The spelling in the recipes is unchanged.

* * * * * * *

I

WE INTRODUCE
DR WILLIAM KITCHINER MD

William Kitchiner Senior, William's father, had come from Hertfordshire to work as a porter in a London coal wharf. By hard work and later by trading as a coal merchant he eventually made a fortune, enabling him to live in great style. His rise from humble coal porter to rich entrepreneur came about because wood was becoming expensive and people were turning to coal as a cheaper means of fuel. Coal came to his wharf by ship from Newcastle and Sunderland, and from there it was delivered to London customers. In the Gordon Riots of 1780, the area round Beaufort Buildings in the Strand, which he had bought, was filled with soldiers to protect the coal wharf in the rear by the riverside. At the same time, the American War of Independence was being fought, and there was a natural build up of militia in the capital city. William Kitchiner supplied coal to the soldiers.

In Boswell's Life of Johnson there is a very good description of the vandalism at the height of the riots:

On Friday, the good Protestants met in St George's Fields, at the summons of Lord George Gordon, and marching to Westminster, insulted the Lords and Commons, who all bore it with great tameness. At night the outrages began by the demolition of the mass-house by Lincoln's Inn. On Tuesday night they pulled down Fielding's house, and burnt his goods in the street. They had gutted on Monday Sir George Savile's house, but the building was saved. On Tuesday evening, leaving Fielding's ruins, they went to Newgate to demand their companions who had been seized demolishing the chapel. The keeper could not release them but with the Mayor's permission, which he went to ask; at his return he found all the prisoners released, and Newgate in a blaze. Then they went to Bloomsbury and fastened upon Lord Mansfield's house, which they pulled down; and as for his goods, they totally burnt them. They plundered some Papists, I think, and burnt a mass-house in Moorfields the same night. On Wednesday they broke open the Fleet, and the King's Bench, and the Marchalsea, Wood Street Compter, and Clerkenwell Bridewell, and released all the prisoners.

The riots were started by a protestant fanatic, Lord George Gordon, who marched with a mob to Parliament to demand a repeal of the Relief Act, which allowed Catholics to own land. Traditional hatred of the catholics, and general discontent among the poor had existed in London for several centuries. Members of Parliament made no decision, and so the frustrated and angry Protestants vented their fury on the properties of well-known Catholics.

The riots lasted for a week. Soldiers were dispatched to quell the rioters, and 'individuals were hunted in their holes, and led to prison; whilst Lord George Gordon was sent to the Tower.' Several hundred people had died in the week of fury, and many rioters were caught – twenty of them eventually being hung.

William Kitchiner was a Justice of the Peace for Westminster and occasionally sat at Bow Street Court House. He was certainly a magistrate at the time of the riots as there is a letter of his dated September 17th 1781, one year afterwards. He describes seven prisoners 'much dissatisfied being charged on account of the Riot'. It was addressed to the Chairman of the Court of Sessions.

After his death on the 19th July 1794, William Kitchiner was buried in the family vault at St Clement Danes Church, London, and left his son a fortune: £60,000 to £70,000, a large sum for those days. Young William Kitchiner was only nineteen years old when he became financially independent.

The only reliable details we have of the first twenty-four years of Dr Kitchiner's life amount to three dates – his birth, the death of his father, and his marriage. William Kitchiner was born in 1775 at Beaufort Buildings, Strand, London. As a very young boy of five he might have seen the Gordon Riots outside his father's house in the Strand and the soldiers protecting his father's coal wharf at the back of the house.

It was widely believed that William Kitchiner had been educated at Eton, where during a game of darts, he was wounded in the eye and lost the sight of it. After a speedy recovery he went back to Eton

The Gordon Riots. Detail from a print showing the burning and plundering of Newgate setting the felons at Liberty by the Mob.

wearing a monocle and his fellow students gave him the nickname 'quiz-fish' (sic). He enjoyed all the sports at Eton College but was determined to make his name in medicine.

He then studied at the University of Glasgow where he obtained his degree only to find out that it was not recognised in England and he could not practise in London.

On 2nd August 1799, at the age of twenty-four, Dr Kitchiner married Miss Oram. The Gentleman's Magazine (September 1799) under Marriages of Remarkable Persons has this simple entry:

> Aug 2 Wm Kitchiner, Esq, of Beaufort-buildings, Strand, to Miss Oram.

This marriage was not successful and the couple parted after only three months. Nothing more was ever heard of Mrs Kitchiner, not even in her husband's Will, though she was certainly still alive at his death.

Dr Kitchiner's home at 43 Warren Street was adjacent to Fitzroy Square. In 1790-94 the east and south sides of this square were built by Robert and James Adam who also built much of the best of London's Georgian domestic architecture. They had been commissioned by the Fitzroys, who were the Dukes of Grafton and owners of the manor of Tottenham Court (where Kitchiner also owned property). Grand new houses and streets were being built and Hepplewhite and Chippendale furniture was in demand.

The Warren Street house no longer exists but was described as sumptuous. Outside the front door Kitchiner would have seen sedan chairs, still the most popular form of urban transport, passing every day to and from the clubs or the theatres. Iron wheeled open carriages would rattle over the filthy street outside his house taking well dressed ladies with parasols to the parks in summer. Dandies with their malacca walking canes strutted along the pavement, and costermongers peddled all manner of wares from rabbits to bread, and trinkets to dog collars. Kitchiner mentions the fish sellers in particular with their cries of 'fresh dainty salmon', 'delicate salmon', 'live cod' and 'new mackerel'. London was just as noisy and raucous then as now.

Despite the elegance of Regency London, public health and hygiene were non existent. Such plumbing as there was would be found only in luxury houses, and there was no proper sanitation; all water for cooking was suspect and had to be boiled, and milk so frequently adulterated that it could be dangerous to drink. Food-poisoning was rife, and because medicine was still in its infancy, deaths were common. Drug addiction among children was a cause of concern, and drunkenness among adults, owing to the vast number of gin-shops, was so bad that several notable artists, including Hogarth, drew attention to this social disgrace in their pictures. Dickens gives a harrowing and vivid description of London's poor in Sketches by Boz:

> We will endeavour to sketch the bar of a large gin-shop, and its ordinary customers, for the edification of such of our readers as may not have had opportunities of observing such scenes; and on the chance of finding one well suited to our purpose, we will make for Drury Lane, through the narrow streets and dirty courts which divide it from Oxford Street, and that classical spot adjoining the brewery at the bottom of Tottenham Court Road, best known to the initiated as the 'Rookery'.
>
> The filth and miserable appearance of this part of London can hardly be imagined by those who have not witnessed it. Wretched houses with broken windows patched with rags and paper, every room let out to a different family, and in many instances to two or even three; and red-herring vendors in the front parlours, and cobblers in the back; a bird fancier on the first floor, three families on the second, starvation in the attics, Irishmen in the passage, a 'musician' in the front kitchen, and a charwoman and five hungry children in the back one – filth everywhere – a gutter before the houses and a drain behind them – clothes drying and slops emptying from the windows: girls of fourteen or fifteen with matted hair, walking about barefooted, and in white greatcoats, almost their only covering; boys of all ages in coats of all sizes, and no coats at all; men and women in every variety of scanty and dirty apparel, lounging, scolding, drinking, smoking, squabbling, fighting and swearing.

Fashionable Londoners strolled and took the air in the Vauxhall Pleasure Gardens, while others flocked to the smart new London shops like Swan and Edgar in Regent Street, Fortnum and Mason, Debenhams, and Hatchards, all recently opened.

Dr Kitchiner took a mistress, Elizabeth Friend, and lived with her for the rest of his life. By her he had an illegitimate son, William Brown Kitchiner, who was born on 23rd June 1804. We have found many references to him mainly concerning his education, but no further mention of his mother, Elizabeth Friend, anywhere except in Kitchiner's Will of 1826, so we can only presume that she took no active part in Kitchiner's social life.

At this time being a bastard was considered a social disgrace, and

William Brown Kitchiner was never to forget his illegitimate status. His father gave him the best education he could, and sent him to Charterhouse School in Surrey from January 1818 till July 1822, then to St. John's College, Cambridge in 1824. However, the son riled his father by trying to disgrace him at every opportunity. In the Dean's Book of 1826, for example, there are a fair number of disciplinary black marks; irregularity in chapel, coming in after 1 am and a sign which means gross ignorance. He studied the classics and other varied and diverse subjects including Mechanics, Calculus, Optics, and Hydrostatics. The study of optics was interesting, and it is possible that Kitchiner was planning to set his son up in an optical business. He was already selling spectacles from his home and other outlets, and it seemed an excellent idea for his son to follow him into the business.

William Brown Kitchiner's College record was most unimpressive. In his first year, 1824, he was in the first class, but by 1825 had dropped to the third class. In his third year he had dropped further to the fourth class, and at the examination in December 1826, he was excused attendance through illness. He did not gain a degree and was also 'very ignorant in every subject of the examination'. He was clearly a great disappointment to his father.

Dr William Kitchiner MD

II

THE COMMITTEE OF TASTE

Dr Kitchiner entertained his friends on a regular basis. Of the two most important of these occasions, the first was a *conversazione* held at his home on Tuesday evenings. This was a gathering of friends to discuss topics of interest and to have supper afterwards. As the first three guests entered his drawing room, he received them seated at his grand pianoforte, and struck up with 'See the Conquering Hero comes'. For this performance, he usually wore silk stockings and pumps and had a contrivance underneath his pianoforte so that he could provide a drum and triangle rhythm worked with his feet. To make sure that the evenings went smoothly, Kitchiner used to fix a placard over his chimney piece, inscribed:

'At seven come, – at eleven go.'

The invited guests for *The Committee of Taste* would meet to taste the food Dr Kitchiner or his cook had prepared, then comment upon it. One of his maxims was that every recipe in *The Cook's Oracle* had been tried by The Committee.

Dinners were announced by 'notes of preparation', which could not fail to excite the liveliest sensations in the epigastric regions of the 'thoroughbred grand gourmands of the first magnitude' who were honoured with the invitation. One of these notes is well entitled to preservation as a curiosity:

Dear Sir,

The honour of your company is requested to dine with the Committee of Taste, on Wednesday next, the 10th instant. The specimens will be placed upon the table at five o'clock precisely, when the business of the day will immediately commence.

I have the honour to be, your most obedient servant, August, 1825.

43, Warren Street,
Fitzroy Square.

In typical Kitchiner style, these invitations were closed with a handsome seal of scarlet wax impressed with the sigillum of *The Committee of Taste*, bearing the motto 'BETTER NEVER THAN LATE'. Guests honoured with such an invitation had twenty-four hours in which to reply, or they were deemed not to be interested. Furthermore, those guests who accepted had to arrive on time, because a few minutes after five o'clock the street door was closed and locked. To emphasise this point Dr Kitchiner continues in *The Housekeeper's Oracle*, (1829):

'As soon as the first course is served the table shall be garnished with the key of the street door.'

At this point the serious business of eating commenced for *The Committee of Taste*. Kitchiner includes an amusing anecdote in *The Housekeeper's Oracle*, which was to have been the companion volume to *The Cook's Oracle*:

A sensible old gentleman when he answered an invitation to dine plainly stated in a *Nota bene* something to the following effect:
Nota bene I conclude you mean what you say, and that dinner will be on the table at five o'clock, when I shall arrive at your door; – if the dinner be on the table – I shall come and partake of it – if it is not – I shall take the liberty of returning home.

At these little social meetings the signal for supper was invariably given at half past nine. All who were not in need of further refreshment would then retire; and those who remained descended to the parlour to partake of the friendly fare, according to the season of the year. As these parties consisted of eminent people of that era the orderly habits of the Doctor were recognised, and, at the appointed time, some considerate guest would observe 'Ah, 'tis on the strike of eleven.' Hats and cloaks, coats and umbrellas were brought in, the Doctor escorted his friends to the street door, looked up at the stars, if there were any visible, gave each of his friends a cordial shake of the hand, wished him a hearty goodnight, and so the evening was ended.

In *The Housekeeper's Oracle* we found a wonderfully pedantic entry relating to a meeting of *The Committee of Taste*. At the last General

The East Side of Fitzroy Square

Meeting of the committee it was unanimously resolved that:

1) An Invitation to ETA BETA PI must be answered in writing as soon as possible after it is received within twenty-four hours at latest reckoned from which it is dated. Otherwise the Secretary will have the profound regret to feel that the invitation has been definitely declined.

2) The Secretary having represented that the perfection of several of the preparations is so exquisitely evanescent that the delay of *one minute* after the arrival of the meridian of concoction will render them no longer worthy of Men of Taste, therefore to ensure the punctual attendance of those illustrious gastrophologists, who on grand occasions, are invited to join this high tribunal of taste, for their pleasure and the benefit of their country, it is irrevocably resolved that the janitor be ordered not to admit any visitor of whatever eminence of appetite after the hour which the Secretary shall have announced that the specimens are ready.

There was another instruction on the invitation stating that the guest had to leave by 11pm or he was not asked again! We learned this particular piece of information from Dr Cock's letter which is reproduced in Chapter 4. Punctuality was very important to Dr Kitchiner, to the extent that all the meals in his house were served on the hour or half hour, invariably to the sound of a striking clock.

Kitchiner's views on prompt dining were well known and respected, and, in our opinion, quite correct. This is what he writes in *The Housekeeper's Oracle:*

Many silly people order the dinner not to be dished up till the last visitor perhaps half to three quarters of an hour after the stated time arrives, yet, for all that, poor Cookey's dishes are expected to look as beautiful and as pretty as if just finished and sent from the fire. It is morally impossible for any cook to have a chance of giving you any dinner fit to be eaten unless you tell her to send it up when it is ready, not matter whether every or any person is present, and not to wait one moment beyond the time.

Can anything be more insulting to those who have come at the time you have requested, than to keep a dozen of such good people waiting and have your dinner spoiled into the bargain because some stupid brute who happens to have more money or less wit than the rest of your guests, choose to rudely neglect coming at the appointed hour?

William Jerdan gives an interesting insight into one of these

Committee of Taste dinners which he attended and comments upon the rumours suggesting how bizarre and strange these dinners were. This account is from his book *Men I Have Known:*

> The dinners at which he entertained a few of his intimates (generally six or eight at the most) were by no means so bizarre as rumour gave them out. If the oddities were there, there was always a fair counterbalance of the relishable and genuine. The very incongruities gave a zest to the treat. A tureen of soup, indeed, was not liked the better for having its ingredients explained, and the price perhaps sixpence or sevenpence recorded (though, after all, it was fairly palatable and nutritious); but at any rate, it might be followed by a costly cut of a Severn salmon, and there was generally a joint, to save you experimenting on made dishes, which, I must own, seemed often to be of dubious quality, and rather dangerous to depend upon for a man with an appetite.
>
> The wines were of sundry kinds, and might be classed as good, bad and indifferent: some especially recommended because they were quite new – fresh from the docks – or tawny from antiquity, or mellowed by age, or having a peculiar bouquet, or 'having eaten up their crust'. Fortunate it was at these meetings that the rule was *de gustibus non disputandum*, every one took what he most fancied, and did what he liked.
>
> Sometimes there might not be that ready overflowing supply which was more usual in those times than in our more temperate days, and the Doctor was deprived of his horizontal constitutional siesta for one hour after dinner. Sometimes mirthful jests were perpetrated, which might remind us of Peter Pleydell's high jinks, described by Sir Walter Scott.
>
> Let it also be remembered that these were but the occasional relaxations of busy men.

The Doctor was especially proud of his coffee. He arranged for it to be roasted – then straightaway ground – then immediately made into coffee as it was required, so as to extract the most flavour and fragrance from the beans. He would never consider drinking nor offering to his guests coffee made from beans that had been pre-roasted at some undetermined date.

Being independent of his profession, he opened his hospitable doors to a wide circle of friends distinguished for genius and learning, and the following people were among the known circle of his friends:

Dr John Haslam, (1764-1844) who was Kitchiner's most intimate friend and a great humorist. He was created a Doctor of Medicine by the University of Aberdeen in 1816, and specialised in psychiatric disorders, writing largely on problems of insanity. After a long and very distinguished career, he died at 56 Lamb's Conduit Street, London.

Samuel Rogers (1763-1855) who may have encouraged Kitchiner in his writing, was another frequent visitor. As a poet he had published many works of his own, including a comic opera, and wrote for *The Gentleman's Magazine*. Like Dr Kitchiner, he was wealthy, and received £5,OOO a year from his share in the family banking business, achieving some notoriety for the lavish breakfasts which he gave. He had a wide circle of friends of his own, many of whom were poets, and some would probably have been introduced to Kitchiner, among them Byron, Coleridge, Keats, Shelley and Wordsworth. During the *Committee of Taste* dinners Samuel Rogers would almost certainly have discussed William Blake, who was both poet and artist, and other great contemporary painters such as Turner, Constable, Zoffany and Stubbs would likewise have come under scrutiny. Samuel Rogers was offered the post of Poet Laureate but he declined the honour.

Charles Mathews (1776-1835) was a celebrated English comedy actor and comedian. He made his debut in 1793 as an actor, but in 1818 decided to leave the legitimate stage and became an entertainer, twice travelling to America. His wife wrote memoirs of him in four volumes in 1839. Theodore Hook had begun a biography of Mathews, but never completed it.

Theodore Hook (1788-1841) was a novelist, miscellaneous writer, humorist, practical joker, and must have been one of Kitchiner's most enigmatic guests. He was educated at various private schools including Harrow, where, according to his own account he 'was principally distinguished for mischief, deceptiveness, and an inaptitude for serious application'. While still a teenager he wrote the lyrics for some of his father's comic operas, and was thus introduced into the world of the theatre. He then produced a number of farces and melodramas, one of which *Tekeli* was ridiculed by Byron, though the public appeared to enjoy the work.

The most famous of his practical jokes took place in 18O9 and became known as the Berners Street Hoax. A Mrs Tottenham had incurred Hook's displeasure, so to wreak revenge on the hapless lady, Hook sent out a reputed four thousand letters to various people including the Lord Mayor of London, chimney sweeps, draymen and the Duke of Gloucester, summoning them on various pretexts to Mrs Tottenham's house in Berners Street. Mayhem was created when everyone turned up and the street was blocked for a day.

In 1813 a brief spell as the Accountant-General and treasurer of Mauritius (a post offered him through connections with the Prince Regent) proved his ruin, as a large sum of money had gone missing. His property on the island was confiscated, and he was sent home. There were no grounds for criminal liability against him, but he was held responsible for the repayment of the debt. His property in England was seized as part payment, the remainder of the debt being allowed to lie dormant for the rest of his life.

Eventually, the Treasury discovered Hook's position and pressed him for the repayment. He wrote nine novels which were successful, but later literary money-making schemes faltered, and upon Hook's death in 1841, a nasty shock awaited his relatives, for the treasury made its claim on the outstanding Mauritius debt.

In Vanity Fair, Thackeray modelled 'Mr Wagg' on Theodore Hook, and Coleridge described him as 'as true a genius as Dante'.

Sir Joseph Banks (1743-1820) who sailed with Captain Cook on his first great voyage in the *Endeavour*, was President of the Royal Society for forty-one years from 1778, and was made a member of the French Institute in 1802. He was also a founder member of the Botanical Gardens at Kew, near Richmond in London, and responsible for bringing some seven thousand new plants into Britain. In the latter part of his life Sir Joseph Banks was to become one of Kitchiner's friends and a frequent guest at the *The Committee of Taste* dinners, when they would have discussed exotic vegetables, herbs and spices. It was he who, when he heard that Kitchiner was planning to write a cookery book, offered to lend his chef Henry Osborne to help. Henry Osborne not only assisted in writing *The Cook's Oracle*, but provided several most interesting recipes.

Sir Joseph was a very conceited person, conscious of his own importance. He refused to sail with Captain Cook on the second great voyage because there was no room on board for his personal entourage of thirteen people, including musicians to play for him as he dined each evening. The sticking point came over the trumpeters. He could not manage with fewer than two. To celebrate Sir Joseph Banks, a four million pound building was opened in 1990 at Kew Gardens and was named after its illustrious founder.

William Jerdan (1782-1869) was a popular journalist and Editor of the *Literary Gazette* for some thirty years. He had suffered severe financial hardship when the privately owned Whitehead's Bank collapsed in 1808, and later, a dishonest friend defrauded and ruined him. However, his skill as a journalist restored his fortunes and he

The Committee of Taste. George Cruikshank

wrote about Kitchiner in his book *Men I Have Known*, three years before he died.

Charles Kemble, (1775-1854) actor, exactly the same age as Kitchiner, became the owner of the Covent Garden Theatre in 1820. He was a member of a renowned theatrical family; Sarah Siddons, the most famous actress of the day, was his sister. Kemble was also a prodigious drinker, to the extent that his doctor told him to give up wine. However, the advice was ignored by him, and he lived to the fair age of seventy-nine despite his drinking habits.

John Braham (1774-1856) was the orphaned son of German Jews, and had been brought up by 'a near relation'. He had known very hard times, once having to sell pencils in the street. He had a marvellous voice, and was well known as a boy soprano, later becoming the most famous tenor of his age and travelling to many countries. Braham and his wife had a great interest in food, and entertained Kitchiner on many occasions in their home in Baker Street, with Mrs Braham frequently swopping her special recipes with him.

During his forty years as a famous tenor Braham had accumulated a fortune. Unwisely, in 1831 he bought the Colosseum in Regent's Park for £40,000, and in 1835 built the St James's Theatre which cost £30,000. Both speculations proved disastrous, and he had to return to the concert hall to restore his finances.

George Colman the younger (1762-1836) took over the Haymarket Theatre from his father and wrote the comedy *The Heir at Law* in 1808. He was appointed Examiner of Plays in 1824.

Charles Dibdin the younger (1768-1833) was the illegitimate son of Charles Dibdin senior. He was a close friend of Kitchiner, and was also proprietor and acting manager of Sadler's Wells Theatre, for which he wrote many plays and songs. One of his best known comic operas was *The Farmer's Wife* written after 1814.

Sir John Soane (1753-1837) was the architect who rebuilt the Bank of England. He was elected to the Royal Academy in 1802. His house in Lincoln's Inn Fields, together with all its art treasures was presented to the nation, and now forms the Soane Museum. Soane was a trusted confidant of Kitchiner.

Hans Busk the Elder (1770-1862) was descended from wealthy Norman aristocracy. He was a landowner, a justice of the peace, and a high sheriff. He was best known for his poetry, and published several volumes of verse including *The Banquet* (1819). However, what is more interesting to us is that he was the proof reader for Kitchiner's various and diverse manuscripts, and in this capacity suggested many improvements to the Doctor's original text. Busk was the father of Mrs Pitt Byrne whose lovely book *Social Hours with Celebrities* has been such a great help to us.

There were other notable people in Kitchiner's life who may have been *The Committee of Taste* dinner guests at some point. One such person was Phillip Hardwick (1792-1870), architect and executor of Kitchiner's Will who later designed the new hall for the Goldsmith's company, and Euston and Victoria stations with their hotels. Another was Thomas Hood (1799-1845), friend of Kitchiner and a great humorist and miscellaneous writer. He wrote the burlesque *Ode to Dr Kitchiner* and included him in his *Whims and Oddities* (1826).

One of his most famous guests was the Prince Regent. It was not long before Dr Kitchiner's reputation reached his ears, and he became a dinner guest at that illustrious table. It was not so much the food that attracted him, as he could probably eat much better at Carlton House, but rather the guests that Kitchiner gathered round him. Though we feel it is unlikely that he attended the formal *Committee of Taste* dinners, probably coming as Kitchiner's private guest on less formal occasions. The reason for this was that at *The Committee of Taste* dinners, which were well organised, the Doctor's guests knew his foibles, and were used to his routines. They knew when to sit down and when to leave. However, even Kitchiner, at the height of his fame, was not in a position to tell the future King when to depart. Through entertaining the Prince Regent, he gradually acquired the nickname of 'Royal Cook', and his fame increased even more.

One reason for the Prince Regent's interest in Kitchiner was not difficult to see. Earlier, as the Prince of Wales, he loathed his father George III, and had married a Roman Catholic widow, Mrs Fitzherbert. His debts were rising, and Parliament told him he had to marry a Protestant princess before they would accept responsibility for them. Reluctantly he agreed.

The disastrous marriage to Caroline of Brunswick took place in 1795, the Prince having to drink himself into a stupor before he could attend the ceremony. The couple were miserable together and separated after the birth of their child, the Prince seeking solace in extravagant living and in food and drink.

The Doctor's own dinners – unless he had special parties – were comparatively plain and simple, served in an orderly manner, and placed upon the table invariably within five minutes of the time announced, which was usually five o'clock. His supper was served at half past nine and at eleven he was accustomed to retire.

Charming well again. A political cartoon showing the Prince Regent partaking of the lightest of meals during his convalescence, 1816.

Dr Kitchiner was convinced that health depends to a great extent on the proper preparation of food, and there were times when he considered his own consumption of animal food excessive. This craving was not to be repressed, nor easily to be satisfied. It had nothing to do with the love of eating, but, he believed, was the result of some organic and incurable disease. His hours of rising, of eating, and of retiring to bed were all regulated by system. He was accustomed to make a good breakfast at eight. His lunches, to which only the favoured few had the privilege of an invitation, were superb, and consisted of potted meats of various kinds, fried fish, savoury pâtés, rich liqueurs, all in great variety and abundance. Though he was unique in London with his *Committee of Taste* dinners, a contemporary cookery writer in France, had organised a similar 'Jury of Tasters', for a totally different reason.

Grimod de la Reynière (1758-1838) was a wealthy French barrister who took more interest in food than the law. As a French aristocrat living through the Reign of Terror in Paris he ran a great risk of the guillotine. However, he had not the slightest interest in politics, and had been born with a deformity; his back was slighty hunched, and he had small webbed hands which he usually covered with gloves. These may have helped him pass unscathed. The story of the deformity is refuted in *Le Memorial de la Pâtisserie* by Pierre Lacam, 1895, who writes about Grimod's several biographers:

> They are all wrong. This malady was the result of an accident. When very young, he was attacked by a ferocious pig. People arrived just in time to rescue him from the teeth of the animal, but by this time his hands had been already eaten. His hands were thereupon virtually useless. However, this did not prevent him from becoming a great writer.

Our belief is that Grimod was, in fact, born deformed, and the story about the mutilation by a pig was probably concocted by his parents to explain his gross affliction. Grimod became a great publicist, and, like Kitchiner, took a mistress – Mlle Feuchère, who sang at the Opéra. At the end of the French Revolution, Grimod set up a *Jury of Tasters*, who met regularly in his house in the Champs Elysées in Paris. Local tradesmen would send him recipes, or actual dishes, which would then be tried out by the Jury. If successful, they received Grimod's *légitimation* which was rather like a seal of approval. These were then given to the tradesmen so that customers would buy goods from them. This was highly successful to begin with, but when it was discovered that Grimod's *légitimation* was given

Grimod de la Reynière

to every recipe or dish submitted regardless of quality, the Jury of Tasters swiftly lost its authority and was disbanded.

Grimod de la Reynière wrote two famous though now obscure works. The first of these, the *Almanach des Gourmands* was virtually Grimod's Food Guide of the times, and eight volumes were published between 1803 and 1812. In this work he praised good restaurants and criticised bad ones, thus acquiring a great reputation as a gourmet and culinary authority, and influencing French cuisine for a large part of the nineteenth century.

Grimod's second work, the *Manuel des Amphitryons*, was written in 1808 and was intended to instruct the nouveaux riches in post Revolution Paris in culinary matters. 'Amphitryon' means 'dinner-giver' and Grimod felt it his duty to teach these coarse eaters table etiquette. For example, napkins should not be knotted round the neck or tucked into one's collar, but delicately laid in one's lap, and he gave directions for place settings comprising several glasses, a meat plate, a fork to the left of the plate, and a spoon and knife to the right. This became the basis of the place setting that we all know today.

Grimod's works were never translated into English, so Kitchiner must have understood the French text, as he mentions 'Monsieur Grimod' in *The Cook's Oracle*, and includes several quotes from the *Almanach des Gourmands*.

We wondered why Kitchiner had chosen Wednesdays for his *Committee of Taste* dinners, rather than any other day. It is quite possible that this was the day when most of his friends would have been free, being mid-week; but there was a much more interesting precedent. In 1779, when Grimod de la Reynière was twenty-one he joined *La Société des Mercredis* in Paris. Members of this exclusive dining club met every Wednesday for a sumptuous dinner in a Paris restaurant, and the club remained in existence until about 1813. The Club is mentioned in Grimod's writings, so Kitchiner would certainly have known of its existence.

Sadly, Grimod de la Reynière is remembered nowadays only in academic culinary circles, which we think is a great pity, for he was such a colourful character.

The Committee of Taste dinner held on February 20th, 1827, was to be the last. Among the guests was Braham, the tenor, as well as Hans Busk. As they all laughed and joked and enjoyed the Doctor's food and hospitality, little did they know that in six days' time the Doctor would be dead.

* * * * * *

III

THE WRITER

Dr Kitchiner's known writings were produced in the last sixteen years of his life, which was clearly a very fruitful and productive time for him.

His first two books were *The Companion to the Telescope* published in 1811, followed by *Practical Observations on Telescopes* which appeared in 1815. He also submitted to *The Philosophical Magazine* an essay on 'Size best adapted for Achromatic Glasses: with hints to Opticians and Amateurs of Telescopes in General'. These erudite works created such a sensation that Kitchiner's fame as an amateur optician was established. But his masterwork was *Apicius Redivivus or The Cook's Oracle.* Here are three testimonials to this work which we found in his *Traveller's Oracle* (1827).

> The *Cook's Oracle* was considered as the *ne plus ultra* of the science of eating, the *crème de la crème* of pure excellence in culinary literature. So much good sense combined with gourmandising – so much plain pot-information conveyed in so truly humorous and original style, place this work on the very eminence of the ample dome of cookery. (*The Monthly Review*, December 1821.)
>
> We venture to prophesy that the *The Cook's Oracle* will be considered as the English Institute of Cookery. (*The Edinburgh Review, 1821.*)
>
> For practical precepts we recommend particularly and chiefly *The Cook's Oracle* in which, along with the plainest directions, there is more of philosophy, and if we may say so of the literature of *gastronomie* than in any work we have seen. (Supplement to *The Encyclopaedia Britannica on Food.*)

Kitchiner had named his cookery book after the Roman *Apicius*. There were, in fact, three Romans of the same name, and all were famed for their gluttony, and feats of gross eating. The first lived in the era of Julius Caesar (44BC), the second taught cookery in Augustus and Tiberius' reign, (27BC-37AD) and wrote a cookery book giving rise to the term 'apician' meaning epicure. The third Apicius lived in the reign of Trajan (98-117AD).

There are notes at the bottom of one or two recipes in *The Cook's Oracle* stating that they have not been tried out by *The Committee of Taste*, and Dr Kitchiner always acknowledges other cooks and professional caterers who contributed recipes. Among these is a Mrs McIver, a Scottish cookery teacher and author who provided a recipe for Haggis, and Kitchiner's own Cook, Elizabeth Lister, contributed several recipes.

Kitchiner was a man with many interests and these filter through into *The Cook's Oracle* making it such an unusual and entertaining book. He tells readers where to buy the best Mock Turtle Soup, and where the best ironmongery shops are in London. He frequently mentions those shops selling very good foodstuffs, for example 'we have bought good Mushroom Catsup at Butler's herb and seed shop, opposite Henrietta Street, Covent Garden.' However, should any *Oracle* reader have gone to Butler's herb and seed shop they would also have seen his bottled Zest Sauce on sale, plus, of course *The Cook's Oracle* – so perhaps the recommendation was not altogether altruistic. He was an astute businessman.

From an historical point of view *The Cook's Oracle* is a treasure house of information, for Kitchiner was an avid reader at all times. He manages to include such interesting snippets of information as, for example, 'at the Spanish Dinner, at the City of London Tavern in August 1808, 400 guests attended for a Turtle Feast, and 2500 pounds of turtle were consumed.' Can you imagine the work involved to produce such a banquet at the start of the nineteenth century, with none of the modern contrivances we all take for granted nowadays?

The public enjoyed the new and freer style of Dr Kitchiner's cookery book, and the critics' favourable testimonials certainly helped to increase the sales, for there were seven editions of the book printed between 1817 and 1840, with reprints virtually every year. In 1821 he wrote *Peptic Precept to Prevent and Relieve Indigestion*, and parts of this were included in later editions.

During 1822 he produced four works of differing subjects. The first two were musical: *Observations on Vocal Music* and *The Loyal and National Songs of England*. In Kitchiner's *The Traveller's Oracle*

(1827) there are sections of several of these National Songs, with the music being composed by him. These were selected from original manuscripts and early printed copies from his own library. Quite often he would play these songs on the piano for his guests and in particular when special ones were present, such as the Prince Regent. The third was *The Art of Invigorating and Prolonging Life by Food, Clothes, Air, Exercise, Wine, Sleep, Etc.* This volume was popular enough to run into four editions, before it finally went out of print. The fourth was *The Pleasure of Making a Will,* ironically, in view of events which were to unfold five years later.

He was a renowned amateur musician, and was also religious, for he composed the music for an English Grace, and describes how he came to write it:

When I last read through The New Testament, I was prompted by the words in the 19th Verse of Chapter X1V of St. Paul's first Epistle to the Corinthians to compose The English Grace.

Bubble and Squeak, or fried Beef or Mutton and Cabbage.—
(No. 505.)

" When 'midst the frying Pan, in accents savage,
The Beef, so surly, quarrels with the Cabbage."

In his recipe for Bubble and Squeak he has composed a little piece based on the musical notation of B E E F and C A B B A G E, which are also the ingredients.

In 1823 Kitchiner completed *A Brief Memoir of Charles Dibdin with some Documents supplied by Mrs Lovat Ashe.* This work relates to a friend of his, Charles Dibdin senior who died in 1814. He had composed many sea songs, and later in life had opened a music shop in London. This was a failure and he suffered bankruptcy. Charles Dibdin then composed twelve songs in 1809 for Dr Kitchiner, who, we believe, would have relished playing these compositions for his guests.

The following year Kitchiner began revising his former work on optics and published it in 1825 under the very lengthy title of *The Economy of the Eyes, Precepts for the Improvement and Preservation of the Sight, and what Spectacles are best Calculated for the Eyes, and an Account of the Pancratic Magnifier.* It was in two parts, the first on the subject in general and on spectacles and opera glasses, and the second part on telescopes. This latter part was based on thirty years experience with the fifty-one telescopes in Kitchiner's possession during 1824-5. He is reputed to have designed all these optical pieces himself, including his 'dumpy' – one of the earliest reflecting telescopes ever made. He certainly did invent his 'invisible opera glass' which he used when travelling in the country. This consisted of a fat walking stick with the inside hollowed out. Down the centre he inserted a very thin twelve inch telescope, so at any time he could raise the walking stick to his eye to examine some far off hill or beauty spot.

Also in 1825 he published *The Housekeeper's Ledger* which included sections on keeping accounts of the expenses of a housekeeper, in addition to Tom Thrift's essay on *The Pleasure of Early Rising.* Then he wrote and completed another new work entitled *The Traveller's Oracle or Maxims for Locomotion,* as well as revising *The Horse and Carriagekeeper's Oracle* written by John Jervis, which was Part Two of *The Traveller's Oracle.* These works were completed but he died before he saw either of them in print.

The public liked and bought this book in sufficient numbers to warrant a second edition. Kitchiner appears to have linked a lot of travellers' stories together, although he never once states that he travelled anywhere we feel sure that as he had inherited his fortune when still a young man, it was likely that he undertook the Grand Tour so customary in the early nineteenth century. There are instructions in the book for travelling by poste or carriage, as well as an indication of the cost of making a journey. He even mentions oilskins for sitting on when enjoying a picnic.

As music played a very important part in his life, Kitchiner included several of his songs in *The Traveller's Oracle,* such as *A Father's Advice to his Son,* among others. His output was prolific and extended to works such as *The Barefooted Friar* (which was a song with three verses, for which he wrote the lyrics as well as the music) and the musical drama *Ivanhoe, or The Knight Templar.* No doubt he would have played most of these compositions at some time or other for his guests at 43 Warren Street, Fitzroy Square.

In 1829 came *The Housekeeper's Oracle or, The Art of Domestic Management*, containing a Complete System of Carving with Accuracy and Elegance, The Art of Managing Servants, Hints Relative to Dinner Parties, and the Economist and Epicure's Calendar. This was a particularly interesting book for two reasons. Firstly, we see William Brown Kitchiner's name on one of his father's books, showing clearly that the son took over the editing and management of the books after his father's death. Secondly, and more importantly, he had intended this book to be a companion to his *Cook's Oracle* – the two volumes becoming a complete book of household management. Kitchiner had written *The Housekeeper's Oracle* specifically for brides, so that they could learn 'the delectable arcana of Domestic Affairs in as little time as is usually devoted to the directing the position of her hands on the Piano-Forte or of her feet in a quadrille'. Thus will 'the cage of Matrimony be as comfortable as the Net of Courtship was charming'.

He mentions sticking plasters for minor wounds to the skin, and he included advice on installing a new invention, what he called a 'stink trap to rid the kitchen of smells'. It is difficult for us in the twentieth century to imagine a sink without a trap but in Kitchiner's day this wonderful new invention showed how elementary the plumbing was.

The Doctor's method of delivery is as engaging as in *The Cook's Oracle*, and there are some wonderful anecdotes. Unlike many wealthy patrons who employed cooks, he frequently did his own shopping and records visits to different tradesmen. When visiting one particular bakery, for example, he records seeing a worker mixing dough with his feet. Although this may seem disgusting by modern standards, it is worth remembering that all bakers' dough in Kitchiner's time was mixed by hand, and was exceedingly heavy and laborious work. Certain doughs were stiffer than others, and it was easier to pummel these with the feet rather than with the hands. In *The English Bread Book* (1857), Eliza Acton also records that bakers were stamping dough with their feet as late as 1850, one year before the first commercial dough making machines were introduced.

Kitchiner describes seventy seven different types of 'sea coal' coming into London, forty five kinds coming from Newcastle, and the remainder from Sunderland. On one of his frequent visits to the cheesemonger, he recalls the following conversation:

> I can never forget asking a cheesemonger which of two cheeses he thought was the best. 'Why Sir, I will tell you with pleasure – I have no reason for not doing so – for you have a palate, and would choose the best cheese if I did not tell you. But my Dear Sir, I

should not like to be often asked such a question. People in general have so little taste, that if they choose for themselves, it is an even chance that they choose the worst, and you know that is the best they can choose for me.'

In welcoming people with poor taste so that he could sell them all his worst cheeses, and keeping the best for his discerning clients, this cheesemonger seems to have shown sound business sense.

Kitchiner was used to shopping around for the best deals. He was keen to bargain and quotes an excellent suggestion for buying meat very late on Saturdays:

Wholesale or large butchers on a Saturday night in summer will sell upon almost any terms, as the meat, although perfectly good and fit for eating on Sunday would not resist the assault of Captain Green until Monday. Upon these occasions, a fine joint of veal or lamb may often be purchased for 3d or 4d a pound.

'Captain Green' was butcher's slang for the discolouration of veal when kept too long. Shopkeepers could keep what hours they liked, and on Saturdays, butchers were keen to keep open as late as possible in the hope of selling all their fresh meat, as, of course, they had no means of refrigerating it till Monday.

Over years of dealing with all manner of shopkeepers, Kitchiner established his rules for marketing which are very simple and to the point. Here he describes buying on credit:

Remember that he that sells on credit asks a price for what he sells at least equal to the principal and interest of the money for the time he is kept out of it; therefore he who buys on credit pays interest for what he buys.

If you take six months credit you must expect to pay 15 to 20 per cent dearer for your goods. Cash and cash only is the corner-stone upon which the economical edifice can be erected.

He describes the marketing technique of loss-leading which we had always presumed was a modern way of getting customers into a shop. Not so, it was certainly used in Regency London:

Sugar is sometimes sold at an under-rate to get customers for tea, which article is again sold too dear. Great bargains are allowed in ribands and gauzes with a view to allure purchases for silks and laces at an exorbitant price. When the bait has been taken, the price of the cheaper commodity is commonly raised or one of inferior worth is substituted in its place. Choose your tradespeople with circumspection.

He was very harsh on the tricksters who set out to catch the unwary shopper, and despised shopkeepers who gave short measure:

> Every trade has its tricks, and if you challenge those who follow it to a game of catch-who-can by entirely relying on your own judgement, you will soon find that nothing by very long experience can make you equal to the combat of marketing to the utmost advantage – and, after all, to depend on an honest tradesman is the only sure plan. Most of those who advertise to sell cheap live by deception and prey on the innocent as sharks do on the incautious fish. It is the height of folly to lay out your money with such people. Don't suppose they are contented with less profits, on the contrary, they get more by vending sophisticated or inferior articles than the regular dealer does at the regular marketing price. There is a variation of a full 20 per cent and sometimes of double that sum in the quality of almost everything which comes to market. *Adulteration of Food*, Mr Accum, 1820.
>
> If you think you have been imposed upon, never use a second word if the first does not do, nor drop the least hint of such imposition. The only method to induce a tradesman to make an abatement is the hope of your future custom. Pay the demand and deal with the gentleman no more.

The use of the word 'sophisticated' is well worth a second look. In Kitchiner's day the word meant adulterated or sub-standard. It would seem odd to him that 'sophisticated' nowadays is used to mean modern and up-to-date.

His description of butter in the London market of 1817 is quite vivid:

> Consumption in London is 50,000 tons. Cambridge and Suffolk furnish 50,000 firkins each containing 56 lbs. That produced in Essex called Epping Butter is the favourite in this market. There are two kinds of butter: Fresh and the salt. What is termed the Weekly Dorset is the best salt butter. This arrives in town (London) twice a week. It is generally about 3d per pound cheaper than the best fresh butter. It will keep good for a fortnight in summer, and fresh longer in winter.
>
> Carlow Butter which comes in about Michaelmas is about 5d per pound less than fresh butter and will keep good for a couple of months. Butter must be as closely compacted as possible in order to

preserve it from the air. The butter near the joints of the tubs where the air has access to it is always the most rancid. Butter gaugers have a long augur which they thrust through the whole tub, and as they find it uniform or one or two or three different qualities mark the cask 1, 2, or 3. Stone jars are infinitely better machines to keep butter in than the tubs it is usually packed in; and the face of it should be defended from the air by constantly keeping it covered by a quart of strong brine.

Salt butter is sold in firkins in about 60 lbs weight and also in what are termed whole half firkins of about 28 or 30 lbs.

Regular shopping made Kitchiner acutely aware of all aspects of food adulteration and he took every opportunity to expose it in his books:

In London, the Milk is not only subject to these variations; but is generally not only skimmed but thinned with Sky-blue (water) from the Iron-tailed Cow (the pump).

London Cream, we are told, is sometimes adulterated with Milk, thickened with Potatoe-starch, (sic) and tinged with Turmeric: this accounts for the Cockneys, on making an expedition to the country, being so extremely surprised to find the thickest part of the Cream at the top!

The ale of public houses is frequently most abominably adulterated by an addition of the poisonous berry called Cocculus Indicus. It is hardly credible what quantity the druggists import or sell for this purpose. One gram of opium is enough to double the intoxication power of a quart of porter.

When lobsters, crabs or prawns are grown stale, some fishsellers boil them a second or even a third time. Others keep them alive so long that they are in a great measure consumed - then they boil them. The great part of lobsters sold in London are boiled and reboiled every day for a week or longer.

The iniquitous Corn Laws were the cause of a great deal of food adulteration, because they made bread, the staple diet of the poor, expensive. The Doctor points out how this flour was adulterated with alum (a stringent double sulphate of aluminium potassium), chalk and even plaster. He added that alum was often added to wheat to clear the river water which was frequently muddy. Tennyson had doubtless read Kitchiner's works when he wrote of places where 'alum and chalk and plaster are sold to the poor for bread'. Kitchiner would have been pleased to see his efforts of exposing food adulteration rewarded. In 1860 the first Food and Drugs Act was passed by Parliament to try to curb food adulteration, but it was only partially successful, and had to be revised and amended in 1872.

He was, arguably, the first to introduce the reader to the chemistry of food, linking cookery with the stomach, which is, after all, a natural progression. He was also aware of the needs of the cook, so he included in his work advice to servants and people entering cookery as a career. This was at a time when there was in society on the one hand great wealth, yet on the other great poverty. He saw cookery as a means of ameliorating the condition of the poorer class.*

Much more than any other cookery book writer of his time he brought his recipes to life. As you read them you can almost imagine him standing there in his kitchen talking to you out of the pages of his cookery book. Included is a recipe for forty Peristaltic Persuaders, made from Turkey Rhubarb, Syrup, and Oil of Carraway. The subject of laxatives would be unusual in most cookery books, but with Dr Kitchiner, the unusual is the normal. We are not aware of any other cookery book beginning with the instruction 'evacuate before you can accommodate'. This was originally published in his *Peptic Precepts*.

The dose of the persuaders must be adapted to the constitutional peculiarity of the patient, when you wish to accelerate or augment the Alvoline [pertaining to the abdomen] Exoneration, take two, three or more, according to the effect you wish to produce. Two pills will do as much for one person as five or six will do for another. They will generally perform what you wish today without what you hope will happen tomorrow, and are therefore as convenient an argument against constipation as any we are acquainted with.From two to four persuaders will generally produce one additional motion within twelve hours. They may be taken at any time by the most delicate females, whose constitutions are so often distressed by constipation – and destroyed by the drastic purgatives they take to relieve it.

The strong Peppermint or Ginger Lozenge, made by Smith, Fell Street, Wood Street, Cheapside, are an excellent help for that flatulence with which some aged and dyspeptic people are afflicted three or four hours after dinner.

Kitchiner also offers some tongue-in-cheek advice for employers about overeating by servants. Only someone with his optician's interest could think up this idea:

*Dr Alexander Hunter's *Culina Famulatrix Medicinae or Receipts in Modern Cookery*, was published in 1810, and linked food to chemistry, but the book never achieved the popularity of *The Cook's Oracle*.

To guard against la gourmandise of the second table [the food which the servants eat] provide each of your servants with a large pair of spectacles of the highest magnifying power, and never permit them to sit down to any meal without wearing them; they are as necessary and as useful in a kitchen as pots and kettles: they will make a lark look as large as a fowl, a goose as big as a swan, a leg of mutton as large as a hind quarter of beef, and a twopenny loaf as large as a quartern, and as philosophers assure you that pain even is only imaginary, we may justly believe the same of hunger; and if a servant who eats no more than one pound of food, imagines by the aid of the glasses, that he has eaten three pounds, his hunger will be fully satisfied, and the addition to your optician's account will soon be overpaid by the subtraction from your butcher's and baker's.

Before there were copyright laws an author could spend a great deal of time writing and publishing a book, only to have large tracts of it poached by another, less scrupulous, writer or publisher. For instance, in 1822, Mrs Mary Eaton published *The Cook and Housekeeper's Dictionary*. One of her recipes for stuffing for hare is clearly taken from Kitchiner's book. In 1806, *A New System of Domestic Cookery* was published by 'A Lady', (Mrs Rundell), which became a best seller. Part of *A New System of Domestic Cookery* is copied verbatim into Mrs Eaton's 1822 book.

As late as 1956 Eugene Herbodeau, writing in the Introduction to a new edition of Escoffier's *Guide to Modern Cookery* (1907), states:

An enormous number of cookery books are now published, many written without discrimination. The recipes they contain have rarely been subjected to experiment, and for the most part they are copied from other sources and grossly deformed in order to give them some semblance of originality.

There was great rivalry among cookery book writers. Like all others before and since, Kitchiner assumed that his was the best work available on the subject. It was the vogue among cookery authors to abuse each other, and the preface or introduction to their books was the favourite place to do this.

Hannah Glasse writes in *The Art of Cookery made Plain and Easy* (1747), that it was a work 'which far exceeds any thing of the kind ever yet published'.

Mrs Rundell, in the Advertisement in the beginning of her New System of Domestic Cookery says:

As the following directions were intended for the conduct of the authoress's own daughters, and for the arrangement of their table, so as to unite a good figure with proper economy, she has avoided all excessive luxury, such as essence of ham, and that wasteful expenditure of large quantities of meat for gravy, which so greatly contributes to keep up the price, and is no less injurious to those who eat than to those whose penury obliges them to abstain. She makes no apology for minuteness in some articles, or for leaving others unnoticed, because she does not write for professed cooks.

W M Street in *The Frugal Housewife* (1811) which was written for young females says:

In preparing the following work for the press particular care has been taken to select such matter only as has an immediate tendency to cultivate the mind, relatively to the subjects treated. For this reason, we have omitted arithmetic, and all other useless tables and calculations.

Kitchiner continues the theme in *The Cook's Oracle:*

This is the only English Cookery Book which has been written from the real experiments of a housekeeper for the benefit of housekeepers, which the reader will soon perceive by the minute attention that has been employed to elucidate and improve the ART OF PLAIN COOKERY. I hope that the most inexperienced student in the occult Art of Cookery, may work from my Receipts with the utmost facility.

He twice quotes Mrs Glasse's cookery book in a rather derogatory fashion, and says his was the first to have weights and measures (quoting another who made a similar claim.)

Eliza Acton, whose *Modern Cookery* became a classic had her recipes mercilessly pillaged. In later editions of her book she writes:

I must here obtrude a few words of personal interest to myself. At the risk of appearing extremely egotistic I have appended Author's receipt and Author's Original Receipt to many of the contents of the following pages, but I have done it solely in self defence, in consequence of the unscrupulous manner in which large portions of my volume have been appropriated by contemporary authors, without the slightest acknowledgement of the source from which they have been derived.

In 1861 Isabella Beeton published her *Book of Household Management*. She compiled the work of many experts into this work, which

Dr Kitchiner with Telescope

became, probably, the world's best selling cookery book. In the preface to her first edition she writes:

> A diligent comparison with the works of the best modern writers on cookery has also been necessary to the faithful fulfilment of my task.

Mrs Beeton would, without doubt, have had her own copy of *The Cook's Oracle* as she was certainly influenced by it, but went several steps further to include the duties of a mistress of the house, the duties of servants, a chapter on the housekeeper, the natural history of the animals and vegetables used as food, legal memoranda, the doctor, management of children, table settings, napkin folding, carving and so on.

She certainly used Kitchiner's recipes. For example, he had invented a Lemon and Liver Sauce for poultry, which was a most unusual combination. She took this recipe and included it in the first edition of her book where it appears as Liver and Lemon Sauce, with the main ingredients transposed. She also includes a recipe for Indian Curry Powder, which, she says, is founded on Kitchiner's recipe. She seldom gave acknowledgement for recipes poached, so he was highly honoured. In the section on mutton in many of the older editions of *The Book of Household Management* there are verses from Shakespeare, and poems about sheep. It is curious that they are similar to the verses that appear in *The Cook's Oracle* first published forty-four years earlier.

Hannah Glasse was eventually declared bankrupt, her cookery book, together with Mrs Rundell's *A New System of Domestic Cookery*, Kitchiner's *Cook's Oracle*, Eliza Acton's *Modern Cookery* and Mrs Beeton's *Book of Household Management* – all written by authors who were never trained as cooks, are probably famous because they appealed to a much wider readership. Eliza Acton's book was still being printed at the turn of the twentieth century, but of the nineteenth century cookery books only Mrs Beeton's book remains in print to this day, albeit under a different name. In 1960 there was a new edition and the name changed to *Mrs Beeton's Cookery and Household Management*, with a long list of contributors, including well-known cookery writers. We possess both the 1861 and 1960 editions and we have been able to compare them thoroughly. We are not aware of even one recipe from the original 1861 edition that remains after 1960, which we think is very sad.

There is also in existence a fascinating unpublished manuscript which belonged to Kitchiner which he used when writing *The Cook's Oracle*. It contains several hundred recipes as well as instructions on wine-making and preserving, and some medicinal gems such as 'Dr Burgh's Water for the Plague', and a very peculiar recipe for 'Convulsions Fitts or Ricketts' for which one of the ingredients is 'horse dung newly made'. This manuscript belongs to Eric Quayle, who very kindly brought it to our notice.

Had Kitchiner not died so young, and perhaps if William Brown Kitchiner had been as great a character and writer as his father, then, undoubtedly, *The Cook's Oracle* would have remained in print for much longer, perhaps even rivalling Mrs Beeton's *Book of Household Management* as the kitchen 'bible'.

The Cook's Oracle. Cartoon by Thomas Hood.

Dr Kitchiner Conversazione, by George Cruikshank.

IV

THE INNOVATOR

AND

PRIVATE MAN

Dr Kitchiner was always interested in improving the quality of people's lives, and correct diet and proper living conditions were an essential part of his philosophy. While the rich could eat well, the diet of the average working man in England was dull, and the poorest diet of all was that of the English mariner. Fifty years before Kitchiner wrote *The Cook's Oracle*, Captain Cook had known that the ills suffered by his crew were largely the result of poor food and very bad conditions. Cook was at the forefront of the campaign to eradicate scurvy from the navy and improve conditions below decks. In many of the big ships in bad weather, when the gun ports were secured and hatches battened down, officers made their rounds with a silver spoon held up to see how much the foul air tarnished it. When the spoon tarnished too badly it indicated a risk of suffocation and a gun port might be opened.

As Kitchiner knew, a good balanced diet – in particular, fresh food – led to good health. Here is an instance of meat being prescribed to cure an illness, on one of Cook's later voyages:

A few days later, when the 'Resolution' was northward bound Cook's health broke down. He speaks of suffering from a billious collic, but it is easy to see that the incessant strain had taxed his iron constitution.

For several days he was seriously ill, and the ship's surgeon (Mr Pattern) tended him night and day. Fresh meat was prescribed, and duly obtained from the only source on board – a dog belonging to Forster.

The thought of eating a dog might revolt some people, but this is not uncommon in Chinese cuisine. We can find no record of whether Captain Cook enjoyed eating Forster's dog, nor of what resentment Forster may have felt at the loss of his pet, but the cure worked, for Cook soon revived.*

The Rotary Kitchiner Stove

Kitchiner, very aware of the bad cooking facilities at sea, invented a rotary oven for maritime use. This incorporated a novel revolving hotplate turned by a handle, so that a kettle, pot or stewpan could be placed directly above the heat when required. The stove worked well, though the handle got very hot indeed, which would have been a disadvantage. He also invented and marketed a bottled sauce which he called Zest, which could be used at sea and by so doing anticipated the age of convenience foods.

*From *Captain Cook's First Voyage* which took place in between 1768-1771. Kitchiner's friend Sir Joseph Banks went with Cook on this voyage, but not on the second or third one.

ZEST

For Chops, Sauces and Made Dishes

This piquante quintessence of Ragout imparts to whatever it touches a most delicious relish. It awakens the palate with delight, refreshes the appetite and instantly excites the good humour of every man's master, the stomach. Soon made savoury sauce.

Stir two drachms of ZEST into a half pint of melted butter. Let it boil up and strain it through a sieve; or each guest may add it at table like salt, and adjust the vibration of his palate to his own fancy.

Sold at BUTLER'S Herb-Shop, opposite Henrietta Street, Covent Garden. It will keep, for any time, in any climate.

Kitchiner never included a recipe for Zest Sauce in *The Cook's Oracle*, but we have traced an authentic one from *The Dictionary of Daily Wants* which was a Victorian encyclopaedia of household information.

Kitchiner's Zest: A well known sauce used for fish, meat, etc, and made as follows: A pint of claret, a pint of mushroom ketchup, and half a pint of walnut pickle; four ounces of pounded anchovy, an ounce of fresh lemon-peel thinly pared, and the same quantity of shalot and scraped horseradish, an ounce of black pepper and allspice, a drachm of cayenne and a drachm of celery seed. Infuse these in a wide mouthed bottle closely stopped for a fortnight, and shake the mixture every day; then strain and bottle it for use. A large spoonful of this stirred into a quarter of a pint of thickened melted butter, makes an admirable fish sauce. Or the same quantity of the Zest may be mixed with the gravy of cutlets, etc, and will prove extremely savoury.

All through his *Cook's Oracle* Kitchiner makes frequent reference to the conditions of the poor. In cookery books at this time, a section on cookery for the poor was *de rigueur*. But it is most unlikely that the poor ever took much notice of such chapters, because illiteracy was common. Many were quite destitute without enough money even to buy daily food, so luxuries like cookery books were out of the question. Kitchiner knew this; much of his advice was to employers on how to handle staff so that their conditions could improve. For example, female staff were not getting enough wages to make provision for their old age, and many ended up as prostitutes:

Here is the source of the swarms of distressed females which we daily meet in our streets. Ye, who think who to protect and encourage, virtue is the best preventative from vice, reward your female servants liberally.

He continues by suggesting charity by selecting female staff from the *Magdalen*:

Much real information might be effected, and most grateful services obtained, if families which consist wholly of females, would take servants recommended from the *Magdalen*.

The *Magdalen* was a hostel for reformed prostitutes, and the idea of rehabilitating them this way via domestic service was very practical.

He suggests that employers care for their staff by rewarding them well:

I advise you to manage it that servants wages all become due and be paid to them on the regular quarter days - and on Christmas Day, if they are very good, you may give them, at an hour before the time which you dine, a dinner of a turkey and plum pudding. On Lady Day, a sirloin of beef, on Midsummer Day, a quarter of lamb, and on Michaelmas Day, a Goose.

As an employer, he was scrupulously fair. He would never summon a servant who had just sat down to his meal, and interrupt his enjoying it in comfort – and the servants' meals were always good. Everyone knew this rule. However, there was one exception to this, again well known to the servants. If a young servant had transgressed, such as neglecting his duties, or not fulfilling them properly, then, on the first offence he received a friendly but firm word from Dr Kitchiner accompanied by a wry smile. If it happened a *second* time, then he would call up the servant just as that unfortunate person was sitting down to his meal. This punishment was a special reproach, which greatly sharpened the attention in front of his fellow-servants.

He would never ask a servant to perform a task for which he was not trained. For example, there was an occasion when his cook, Elizabeth Lister, came upstairs one morning to tell the Doctor that she needed butter. As it was raining heavily at the time the Doctor asked the coachman to go and fetch a pound of it. However, the coachman, not long in the Doctor's service, complained that 'fetching butter was not a coachman's job.' 'Ay', said his master quietly, 'then put the horses to the carriage and bring it round.' As this was clearly within the province of the coachman's duties, he had to obey the order. The coach arrived, and Kitchiner turned to his cook. 'Now,' he said to her, 'you get in and John will drive you to fetch the butter.' This lesson was not lost on any member of the household staff, and no similar difficulty ever happened again.

Kitchiner was one of the very few wealthy cookery writers who had the good sense to experience what it was like to work as a servant, and find out for himself some of the day-to-day problems in a kitchen. Though he employed a household staff, as can be seen in his Will in Chapter 6, he frequently cooked and experimented with different dishes, and most certainly washed up. Only by doing this could he have made the suggestion that stewpans ought to be curved at the bottom to make them easier to clean. Working in a kitchen also brought him in touch with other cleaning problems:

> Have the dust, etc, removed regularly once in a fortnight, and have your kitchen chimney swept once a month; many good dinners have been spoiled and many houses burnt down by the soot falling - the best security against this is for the Cook to have a long birch broom, and every morning brush down all the soot within reach of it. Give notice to your employers when the contents of your COAL CELLAR are dimished to a chaldron.

A chaldron was a measure often used for coals. It was thirty-two bushels; that is a capacity measurement equal to eight gallons.

He suggested that an oven thermometer ought to be designed to help the cook regulate her oven. Only many years after his death was the oven thermometer invented.

For those who could not imagine what conditions in a large nineteenth century kitchen would be like, Grimod de la Reynière gives a graphic description in his *Almanach des Gourmands*. Like Kitchiner, he had a great sympathy for the chefs and cooks who all too often received little praise for their toils:

> To say nothing of the deleterious vapours and pestilential exhalations of the charcoal, which soon undermine the health of the heartiest, the glare of a scorching fire, and the smoke so baneful to the eyes and the complexion, are continual and inevitable dangers: and a cook must live in the midst of them, as a soldier on the field of battle, surrounded by bullets, bombs and rockets; with the only difference, that for the first, every day is a fighting day, that her warfare is almost without glory, and most praiseworthy achievements pass not only without reward, but frequently without

thanks for the most consummate cook is, alas! seldom noticed by the master, or heard of by the guests; who, while they are eagerly devouring his turtle, and drinking his wine, care very little who dressed the one, or sent the other.

Kitchiner was fully aware of those appalling conditions, and suggested that kitchens should be properly designed:

> Cleanliness and a proper ventilation to carry off smoke and steam should be particularly attended to in the construction of a kitchen; the grand scene of action, the fireplace, should be placed where it may receive plenty of light; hitherto the contrary has prevailed, and the poor cook is continually basted with her own perspiration.

A rich man's London house of the time had a kitchen which was by today's standards extremely basic and modest, being little more than a few basement rooms. The kitchen itself would have a large scrubbed wooden table placed in its centre, and an open fireplace, probably with a clockwork roasting-spit, a Dutch oven, gridiron, copper, butter churn, and so on. Cooking pots were made of iron, silver, or tin-lined copper, and those used for storage were frequently in earthenware. There would have been various cupboards and shelves for storage, and possibly a scullery with a wooden plate-rack and stone sink where dishes and pans would be washed. There would be a larder for keeping meats and poultry, with usually a thick marble slab for making pastry on, and a coal house, or fuel store. Space permitting, there might also have been a still-room for the storage of home-made jams and preserves.

Nowadays, all commercial kitchens have proper ventilation and ducts to take away fumes. Kitchen planning firms abound; kitchen design is a major industry, and we think that Kitchiner would have loved a modern kitchen in stainless steel.

Here we include one of his strangest inventions; his Feet Preservers, which are mentioned in *The Traveller's Oracle*. These were thin insoles 'not above one fifteenth of an inch in thickness' that fitted inside leather boots, and designed as a defence against aching feet on a long walking journey. We do not know how effective these were, nor do we have any records of their use, however there are many such insoles on the market today, so they may well have been quite successful.

* * * * * * *

We tried to find Dr Kitchiner's Eton College records to see whether he showed any developing talents for music, writing or science. We also wanted to check the story about his being blinded in one eye by a dart (which might explain his later interest in telescopes). However, when we wrote to Eton, we were very surprised to learn that he had never been educated there.

Somewhat unsettled by the deception over Eton, we checked with the University of Glasgow, and were, again, very surprised to find that this establishment had no record of Dr Kitchiner as a student, nor had he even been on a register of practitioners. His name does not appear on the University of Glasgow's rolls of graduates or of matriculated students, nor on the separate register of medical students which has been kept at the University since 1802. His name does not appear among the licentiates or members of the Royal College of Physicians and Surgeons.

However, it is just possible that he was a medical student at the University of Glasgow, and left without gaining a degree before records began in 1802. Eric Quayle in *Old Cook Books* (1978) supports this idea:

> On the death of his father, when William was still at University, he had inherited an income of several thousands of pounds a year.

Had he been awarded a degree that would certainly have been recorded. The lack of a medical degree would also explain why he never practised medicine in England.

The information about Eton and Glasgow University was almost certainly supplied to publications such as *The Gentleman's Magazine* by Kitchiner himself. Extracts were then taken from these magazines and periodicals by later writers to form part of his entry in *The Dictionary of National Biography*. He wished the world and the influential society at large to think of him, and accept him at face value, as an old Etonian, and a Doctor, and everyone did. Nobody ever questioned his claims. The addition of MD after his name gave a certain authority to his writings, and probably helped to increase the sales of his books, and so, in effect, became his *nom de plume*.

He was, however, a disappointed man. His marriage had failed, his son was a thorn in his side, and magazines suggested that he was a plagiarist. Yet, despite all this, his public image was one of great enthusiasm for almost everything he embraced, which included games such as chess and whist, for which he enjoyed some reputation. He was much in demand for settling disputes, and though he could easily have afforded the latest style in clothes, he always appeared soberly dressed, unlike the dandies who paraded in the fashionable streets and parks. Mrs Pitt Byrne knew Kitchiner and describes him as follows:

> There can be few living who know as much of Dr Kitchiner as myself . . . . I can see his tall, spare figure with rather small head, high forehead and hair already thinned and turning to grey; his eyes of greyish blue, with their mild but intelligent expression, and the blue-tinted spectacles in slight gold frames that he always wore . . . . His dress I remember well; though somewhat out of date he wore it with elegance; knee breeches and black silk stockings cut steel buckles at the knee bands and the same on low-cut shoes, and frilled shirts. This was still the evening dress of elderly men.

She also added that Kitchiner loved children:

> . . . . his delight was to seat himself at the piano, a child on each knee, and to sing to us the old nursery songs he had set to music, for he was a born musical genius. When he penetrated our nursery it was with his pockets filled with barley sugar 'kisses' folded in little papers of all colours, and after inviting us to dive for them, he would imprison our small hands, and then turn and chase us round the room in a game of romps, which he seemed to enjoy as much as ourselves.

There is an excellent description of Kitchiner in William Jerdan's book *Men I Have Known*:

> Doctor Kitchiner was a character. The march of intellect, as we call it, is treading character out, and it is becoming very rare to meet with a 'real' Original. In elder days (sic), when characters were more plentiful, it was epigrammatically said of another, a dramatic and medical humorist –
>
> > *For Physic and farces*
> > *His equal there scarce is.*
> > *His farces are physic:*
> > *His physic a farce is.*

And so it might be said of Kitchiner (only in prose, the words being intractable to verse), for medicating and book-making he had no equal: his medicating was book-making and his book-making medicating. But his medication was not limited to two or three parts of the system: it was universal. There was no part or portion of the human frame that he did not take under his protection.

Yet there were three especially favoured – the eye, the ear and

In the Kentish Hop Merchant and Lecturer in Optics, Dr Kitchiner is shown giving a lecture on optical matters to a somewhat rustic audience. The Kentish Hop Merchant is not impressed by him.

the stomach; for he was a great optician, a great musician, and a great gastronome. And he was exceedingly good natured with all. Though occasionally a little petulant, he speedily forgave offence, and refraternised with the offender. For instance, when one of his friends ridiculed his optical science, and told him in ancient Latin phrase, about needing the aid Beati Martini (vulgarly rendered 'all me eye and Betty Martin') he saw and laughed at the joke without using his spectacles.

Of his music he never tired; nor did it ever cross his mind that anybody else could resist being 'apt in the elysium of his piano'. His medical ('peptic') precepts and gastronomic practices were wonderfully combined, insomuch that it was not always easy to tell, in partaking of what was set before you, whether you might be swallowing a meal or a prescription at his hospitable, or, as the case may be, his hospital board.

Doctor Haslam, to whom I have referred as the Doctor's intimate friend, was a very skilful mad-doctor, and almost as great a humorist as Kitchiner himself. When *The Cook's Oracle* was published, it so happened that the Editor of a periodical which reviewed new works was in the country, and had left the office of criticising any novelty (in his way) in the charge of the gentleman referred to, than whom there could not be one found in London more competent for the task.

He did perform it in a very entertaining style; but shockingly to disturb the amour propre of the author, who rushed in fury to his bosom friend to seek counsel for implacable revenge. Haslam did not venture to confess the criticism, for the Doctor declared that the injury was of a nature never to be forgiven; and his account of the interview was ludicrous beyond description.

In a few months, however, *The Cook's Oracle* was pacified and reconciled to every member of his *Committee of Taste*, whose praise of his unrivalled gourmetry at the next meeting was potent enough to heal any wounds.

We do not think that the Doctor ever found out that it was his old friend Dr Haslam who wrote the review of *The Cook's Oracle*, and the joke stayed a secret.

On 25 February 1927, *The Times* printed a centenary article entitled 'Doctor and Cook: William Kitchiner 1777-1827' (the incorrect birth year is curious):

Tomorrow will be the centenary of the death of Dr. Kitchiner, who wrote *The Cook's Oracle*, the best cookery book according to modern ideas that has ever been published, because it is the outcome of the medical knowledge of a physician combined with a scientific and practical experience in housekeeping and cookery. So often the man of science can't cook, and the cook knows nothing of science.

Doctor Kitchiner says he 'has considered the Art of Cookery not merely as a mechanical operation, fit only for working cooks but as the Analeptic part of the Art of Physic,' with this result: 'If Medicine be ranked among those Arts which dignify their Professors, Cookery may lay claim to an equal, if not a superior, distinction – to prevent diseases is surely a more advantageous Art to mankind than to cure them.'

A whole-length portrait engraved from a mezzotint represents him as a tall, slight, studious-looking man wearing spectacles, and it is possible that a delicate constitution may have had something to do with his interest in food and its relation to health, and his desire to provide a cookery book for the use of physicians and cooks, for he had scarcely reached 5O when he died. It is something of a coincidence that 1OO years after his death there should be put into force two Acts of Parliament on matters in which he would have been intensely interested - the Pure Food and Weights and Measures Acts. He was a stickler for organised housekeeping, and would most certainly have had all goods weighed before being placed in storeroom or larder.

The following letter appeared in *The Times* a few days later:

Your article on the centenary of Dr William Kitchiner, musician, cook, reformer, and the general repository of the scientific knowledge of his time, brings to mind that I was among the few who saw his translation when the Carey Street burial ground was cleared for the erection of W H Smith & Son's new buildings. He had been buried in a vault on the South side of the cemetery with other members of his family, and I suppose now lies with them at Brookwood. He was a friend of some of my forbears, and I have one of the printed invitations 'to Eta Beta Pie.' You print the heading of such a one, but not the instructions on the bottom. The guest had to answer the invitation within 24 hours or he was excluded. He had to be ready to sit down at 5.OO, and to be in the house before that or again there was no admittance; and lastly he had to leave at 11pm or he was not asked again. Kitchiner is the lecturer in optics in the well-known caricature of the Kentish Hop Merchant, when the old gentleman tells him 'they ain't called Hopsticks but Hoppoles with us.'

Dr F W Cock, Appledore, Kent.

Neither of us knows from where Dr Cock obtained his information. When Kitchiner wrote his Will he expressed a wish to be buried in the family vault in St Clement Danes Church in London. We checked with St Clement Danes, but records prior to 1958 are now kept at the City of Westminster Public Library. We checked with the Archives Department, but nothing could be found. Dr Cock said he saw Kitchiner's body being removed and suggested he had gone to Brookwood. We checked with Brookwood Cemetry in Woking, Surrey, but no trace of Dr Kitchiner could be found.

Part of the old cemetery at St Clement Danes now lies underneath the busy roadway outside the church. Indeed when a bore was taken for an underground line in the area it went through bones and coffins. Our only conclusion is that Dr Kitchiner will lie under the road beside St Clement Danes Church in London for ever.

That he was an imposter does not diminish by one iota our affection for Kitchiner. Here was a man in love with life wishing to embrace every aspect of it to the full. If he told a few untruths about his education, let us forgive him - after all nobody suffered, for he never practised as a doctor, and we are not aware of any other fabricated stories during the rest of his life. He was one of the most famous characters of his age and one of the most talented in cookery, music and optics.

* * * * * *

V

DINNER PARTIES

With the growth of the *nouveaux riches*, the houses of the wealthy came to be treated more as showcases for displaying wealth than for living in. Dinner parties were an excellent way of achieving this, when all the silver, plate, glassware and porcelain could be displayed to great effect, as well as a lavish variety of dishes for the diners. Those guests already on the social ladder would accept the owner as an equal. Those invited from a lower social class could come and admire the possessions on display. However, to give a dinner party required the services of a good cook or chef. More often than not domestic servants were recruited from the poor, often illiterate, working class, and had to be trained to domestic life. As there was no social security then, a domestic position in a good private house was much to be envied, and indeed coveted, as it provided a regular income, a roof overhead, a clean uniform, and, above all, daily food.

But few of the *nouveaux riches* knew how to organise the dinner parties which were now extremely fashionable. Many books on the correct way of entertaining were written to enlighten them. Kitchiner was very scathing about anyone who gave a dinner party for the wrong reason and purely to impress his neighbours. This extract is taken from his *Housekeeper's Oracle*:

> Who does not perfectly understand that a parade of useless plate and a profusion of curious viands and costly wines are not set out so much to entertain the guests as to afford an ostentatious evidence of the opulence, pride and vanity of the host.

His idea of a dinner party was to have few guests, as he had for *The Committee of Taste*, which never numbered more than six or eight. He deplored the extravagance of the 'grand dinner party' when overweight guests ate far too much – particularly when the poor and needy often went without food.

> The old adage that 'the eye is often bigger than the belly' is often verified by the ridiculous vanity of those who wish to make an appearance above their fortune. Nothing is more fatal to true hospitality than the multiplicity of dishes which luxury has made fashionable at the tables of the Great, the Wealthy – and the Ostentatious - who are, often, neither great nor wealthy.
>
> A dinner table should not be more than three feet and a half in width. What will spread handsomely on such a table will appear scanty on a table five feet in width. Provide for one or two more guests than you expect especially if you are not well acquainted with the eating capacity of your visitors, and some folk eat two or three times as much as others do.

At small dinner parties he tells us that it was the duty of the host to introduce all his guests to each other as well as mentioning their pursuits and professions, so that everyone was put at his or her ease. He also suggested using place names for dinner guests so that the host 'will place those together who he thinks will harmonize best'. He describes a new French fashion of seating guests for a small dinner party:

> *Le Journal des Dames* informs us that in several fashionable houses in Paris, a new arrangement has been introduced in placing the company at a dinner table. 'The ladies first take their places, leaving intervals for the gentlemen; after being seated, each is desired to call on a gentleman to sit beside her; and thus the Lady of the house is relieved from the embarassment of etiquette as to rank and pretensions. But without doubt', says the journalist who wrote the piece, 'this method has its inconveniences. It may happen that a bashful beauty dare not name the object of her secret wishes, and an acute observer may determine, from a single glance, that the elected is not always the chosen'.

Kitchiner mentions the 'barbarous manners of the 16th century'. He takes this extract from *The Accomplished Lady's Closet of Rarities, or the Ingenious Gentlewoman's Delightful Companion* (1653):

> A gentlewoman being at table, abroad or at home, must observe to keep her body straight, and lean not by any means with her elbows, nor by ravenous gesture discover a voracious appetite; talk not when you have meat in your mouth; and do not smack like a pig, nor

venture to eat spoonmeat so hot that the tears stand in your eyes, which is as unseemly as the gentlewoman who pretended to have as little a stomach as she had a mouth, and therefore would not swallow her peas by spoonsful; but took them one by one, and cut them in two before she would eat them. It is very uncomely to drink so large a draft that your breath is almost gone and are forced to blow strongly to recover yourself - throwing down your liquor as into a funnel is an action fitter for a juggler than a gentlewoman; this much for your observations in general; if I am defective as to particulars, your own prudence, discretion and curious observations will supply.

Kitchiner planned his *Committee of Taste* dinners so that he could use ingredients of the highest quality. Menus could only be planned a day or so in advance because tradesmen's deliveries could not be guaranteed. In *The Cook's Oracle* he describes fresh fish sometimes taking two weeks to reach London from Scotland because of bad weather.

The joint of meat would have been bought a few days beforehand and be at its most tender; other ingredients were obtained as near to the time of the dinner as possible. But even Kitchiner, despite all his careful preparations, could not forsee every problem in the kitchen. It was quite common for joints of meat to be 'before the fire' for two hours on two different days – and one joint to be almost raw, and the other to be charred (caused by sudden gusts of wind, for many houses were very draughty indeed, a storm overhead causing wind to be sucked up the chimney, or, more commonly the fire not being made up properly by the cook). It took a good chef to compensate for this and regulate his roasting spit accordingly. He comments on the fact that many good joints have been sent to table almost raw because of this problem.

After the French Revolution, many French chefs found themselves without masters. Some set up restaurants in Paris or elsewhere in France; others came to England to work in the houses of the English aristocracy, and with them they brought their French cooking and customs. One of the greatest French chefs to come to England was Antonin Carême 1784-1833, who became famous particularly for his great, almost architectural, confectionery work.

Carême was the Prince Regent's cook for two years, but did not like the London fog. He eventually left the Royal service and returned to France, but the legacy he left, in particular the table centrepieces, or 'pièces montées' became fashionable. Charles Elme Francatelli

1st Course ___Fish Remove

Transparent Soup

Pigeons Compot

Fricasd Chickens

Marrie

Lamb Ears Forced

Pork Griskins

Cidabrows like little Turkey

French Pye

Kidney Beans

Broccoli &c.

Fricando Veal

Boild Turkey

Mock Turtle

Small Ham

Sheep Tongues in Ragout rice

Boild Peas

Sallad

Hare Pie in ala ryal

House Lamb

Larded Oysters

Pistallets

Beef Olives

Florendine of Rabbits

Ducks Alamode

Hare Soup

Remove hanch of Venison

2ᵈ Course

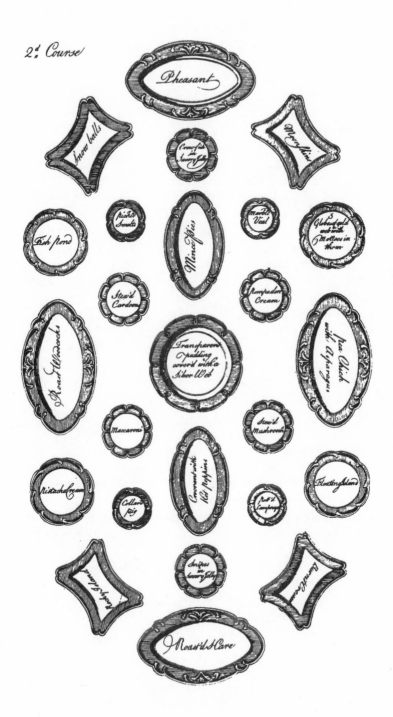

Pheasant

Snow balls   Merryline

Cray fish in Savory Jelly

Fish pond   Pickled Smelts   Mince Pies   Marble Veal   Globes of Gold web with Mottoes in them

Stew'd Cardoon   Pompadore Cream

Roast Woodcocks   Transparent Pudding cover'd with a Silver Web   Pea Chick with Asparagus

Maccaroni   Stew'd Mushrooms

Pistacha Cream   Crocants with Hot Poppins   Pott'd Lampreys   Floating Island

Collar'd Pig

Apricock Cream   Snipes in Savory Jelly   Burnt Cream

Roast'd Hare

writing in *The Royal English and Foreign Confectioner* (1862) gives a wonderful idea of the intricacy of these works of art, prepared for royal or grand occasions. Models such as forts, castles and ruins, would first of all be drawn out on paper to prepare templates. Pastillage (sugar, gum and egg white) would then be made to the size of templates and left to dry before being fitted together. If they had to support fruits, bonbons or other foods, then they frequently had a metal rod through the centre to carry the weight. Other favourites were rocks with spun sugar to simulate a waterfall, swans or other animals, temples, cottages, pavilions and churches. On this subject Francatelli adds 'nothing should be hurried when you are composing any kind of ornament; and it is wrong to attempt anything of the sort, unless you have plenty of leisure time patiently and carefully to carry out your design'.

For everyday cooking, a male French chef, rather than the more common female professed cook, became a status symbol. Those employers who did not have a French chef often sent their cooks to France to learn French cooking, but the 'French' dishes which were then served were rarely authentic. Conversely, some of the English food adopted by the French was far from genuine. For example, Le Rosbif, or Le Roast Beef, often meant roasting any meat, not just beef. Beauvilliers in his book *L'Art du Cuisinier* (1816) lists *Roast Beef of Ardennes Mutton* among dishes on one menu.

George III, who preferred plain and simple food, demanded little from his chefs, so it was quite natural that when the flamboyant Prince Regent (the exact opposite of his father) took over the royal duties, formal dinners became extravagant and almost grotesque in the amount of food provided. Wastage must have been great, though no doubt what food was returned to the kitchen was quickly eaten by the staff. Gradually the English aristocracy adopted the French style of serving dinners, which became known as the 'French dinner', or 'service à la française'.

In the centre of the dining table would be a large floral decoration often incorporating fruit. In addition to this there might be a flummery (from which our blancmange is derived) in the shape of a bird on a nest with some eggs, or a fish swimming in water. If the dinner was to be a very grand affair with a special guest, then there would certainly have been a work in pastillage in celebration of his or her life.

Most formal dinners comprised two courses, but each one of these contained ten or twenty different dishes, all placed on the table at the same time, rather like a buffet. The first course might consist of two or more soups in tureens placed at each end of the decorated dinner table, and the side dishes or hot 'entrées' (which would have lids on to keep them warm) might include salmon and turbot, sweetbreads in a sauce, calves liver, ragouts (casseroles) of veal or beef, lamb cutlets, and items such as mushrooms in a cream sauce.

When the guests had finished the soup, the tureens and the covers from all the 'entrées' were removed. The guests then started eating this intermediate course (called the 'remove') by helping themselves to food from the nearest dishes. Sometimes they asked other guests to pass them food, or they might even request servants to pass them whatever was required.

In addition to all this servants would pass each of the guests 'assiettes volantes' (or 'flying dishes') which might be little fillets of fried sole, or an oyster patty, brought hot from the kitchen. Diners did not eat everything that was in front of them, but instead chose what they fancied from the great variety of dishes on the table. This process was extremely messy, and inevitably pieces of food and dribbles of sauce ended up on the tablecloth, giving the whole appearance of a badly organised cold buffet. As soon as the guests stopped eating, the first course ended and the table was cleared.

The second course would contain the main part of the meal – the 'pièce de résistance' or 'grosse-pièce'. This would be the butcher's meat, such as spit-roasted beef, fillet of veal, boiled leg of mutton, or a joint of glazed ham. These would be garnished and accompanied by a selection of vegetables such as spinach, turnips, Jerusalem artichokes, cauliflower or cabbage. Again, everything for the second course was put on the table at once, so pastries, jellies, burnt creams, russes and cheesecakes would take their place beside the 'rôts' such as the game birds, like mallard, pheasant or widgeon.

Elizabeth Raffald, writing in her delightful book *The Experienced English Housekeeper* (1769), wanted to give her readers a proper sight of the first and second courses of a grand dinner with the table viewed from above. So she commissioned an engraver to make the two copper plates for the illustrations on pages 52 and 53.

Kitchiner describes taking a 'coup du milieu' – which is the equivalent of the modern sorbet eaten in between courses during the meal, rather than a dessert at the end:

There is no French Dinner without soup, which is regarded as an indispensable overture. It is commonly followed by 'le coup d'après', a glass of pure wine, which they consider so wholesome after soup, that their proverb says that the physician thereby loses a

55

fee: whether the glass of wine be so much more advantageous for the patient than it is for his doctor, we know not, but believe it an excellent plan to begin the banquet with a basin of good soup, which, by moderating the appetite for solid animal food, is certainly a salutiferous custom. Between the roasts and the entremets they introduce 'le coup du milieu' – or a small glass of Jamaica Rum, or Essence of Punch, or Curacao. The introduction of liqueurs is by no means a modern custom; our ancestors were very fond of a highly spiced stimulus of this sort, commonly called *Ipocrasse* which generally made a part of the last course, or was taken immediately after dinner.

He always disliked the 'French dinner' as, from the cook's point of view, preparing and serving many dishes at once was very frustrating indeed:

With all your care, you will not much get credit by Cooking to perfection, if more than One Dish goes to table at a time.

At a small formal dinner party there would often be a guest of honour, who might be a friend of the family or a specially invited guest. The guest of honour was so called because he had the honour of carving the roast joint for the other diners. After the meat had been eaten, plates would be removed and fresh ones placed in front of each guest, and the desserts would be eaten. The desserts were termed 'entremets', literally, between-the-courses, for very grand dinners would have a third course which was devoted entirely to work of the pastry chefs, such as ice creams, sometimes in the shape of a boar's head, imitation hams, or a crown, and special pastry confections. Finally fresh fruits, cheese and nuts would be eaten.

Francatelli in his *Cook's Guide and Butler's Assistant* (1861), gives Bills of Fare for every month of the year.

As the cost of maintaining the grand houses increased the kitchens could no longer support a pastry chef, so the third course was dropped in all but the very grandest of establishments and the 'entremets' were placed in the second course. Desserts, fresh fruit and cheeses were frequently omitted from menus at this time, as they were not considered important from the culinary point of view. Some restaurants listed them on separate menus, and this custom is still fashionable today.

In some *nouveaux riches* homes it was also customary to remove the table cloth after the main part of the meal was served. This gave the host a chance to show off his fine polished mahogany or oak dining table. Fine porcelain plates and silver fruit knives and forks were then placed in front of each guest and the dessert was then served. The great Victorian chef Alexis Soyer in his splendid book *The Modern Housewife* (1849), gives a wonderful description of this:

> In order to prolong the time, and to enjoy the gentlemen's society as much as possible, I do not have the dessert placed on the table until ten or twenty minutes after the cloth is removed; this gives an opportunity for my guests to admire the beautiful Sèvres dessert plates, containing views of different French chateaux; this of course gives a subject for conversation to those who have visited them. In the dessert I generally introduce some new importation such as bananas, sugar cane, American lady apples, prickly pears, etc, and these also give a subject for the gentlemen to talk about when the ladies have left, such as free trade, colonial policy, etc. About half an hour after the dessert is on the table, and when I see that the conversation is becoming less general, I retire to the drawing room; the servants then remove the used glass and plate, and Mr B. introduces some of his choice Claret or Burgundy in ice coolers.

The description of claret or burgundy in ice coolers is most interesting being the exact opposite of today's fashion. The pineapple was the fresh fruit in greatest vogue at this time, but Soyer was always looking for more novelties to offer his guests for dessert, such as the fruits mentioned above.

Dinner fashions were undergoing many changes at this time. For the guests 'service à la française' was virtually a self-service meal from the table top, much of the meal being tepid or even cold before it was eaten. Hot sauces which the kitchen staff had prepared and (hopefully) served to perfection would most likely be eaten congealed and cold. By the middle of the nineteenth century the old huge two course buffet-like dinners were giving way to a more delicate, fashionable new style of dinner with the servants bringing round every dish as a separate course. This meant a smaller variety of dishes, but not necessarily less food per guest, as each one was offered every dish. Though this reduced the kitchen stress somewhat, it did mean that the servants had to be skilled in serving food, which was not always the case.

This was known as 'service à la russe'. The dining table was decorated as before with flowers – and some dessert dishes, usually fruit, and the table cloth stayed on for the whole meal. Food was not displayed on the table, but kept on the sideboard, and was then brought round by servants, the dinner guests helping themselves to what they wanted. For one particular dish, one servant would bring round the meat, another the vegetables, and a third would bring a sauce if appropriate.

The principle of 'service à la russe' remains in most high class hotels and restaurants today, although it now incorporates 'silver service', which is the method whereby waiters serve each guest individually using a spoon and fork to lift the food from the salver or dish on to the guest's plate. In modern catering establishments kitchens are usually placed next to the dining room, or restaurant, so that the customer can get his or her food as quickly as possible after it leaves the kitchen.

The 'assiettes volantes' or 'flying dishes' so beloved of the Regency period gradually evolved into hot 'hors d'oeuvres' dishes as a starter, but the cold 'hors d'oeuvres' (now a normal starter in twentieth century dinners) was not always served at the start of a meal. In some French menus it was served after the soup. Lord Palmerston chose to have it after the fish, and for the Duchess of Sutherland's banquets it was served after the 'removes'.

In Russia it was common to have salt herring, anchovies and caviar in an ante-room (together with kümmel) as an appetiser before the dinner started, which makes an interesting comparison with our modern custom of having pre-dinner drinks with 'crudités'.

Soyer Cooking on his Magic Stove (detail).

The problem of cold food was solved by Soyer with his magic stove, as he called it, which was heated by a spirit lamp. It was so successful that he took it to the top of the Great Pyramid in Egypt to demonstrate it working. It started a whole new genre of dishes cooked in front of the guest – 'flambé' cooking! And food could be quickly reheated on the magic stove in the dining room before it went to the guest.

There was always confusion over the titles of courses. What we know today as a roast course was, in Regency times, split into two, often with a sorbet served in between. The 'grosse-pièce' or 'pièce de résistance' would be termed the 'remove' or 'relevé', and were the main part of the meal. The roast or 'rôt' would include the game birds, such as mallards, partridge, or pheasant, which were thought of as much more delicate in taste. To complicate matters even more, fried fish was often included among the 'rôts' in the months when game was scarce. Originally, fish served as a 'rôt' were always served hot, but fashions changed and decorated cold salmon, trout and lobster became acceptable.

There were also additional dishes called 'flancs' at very formal dinners – which Soyer describes in some detail. They 'are only required when eighteen or twenty persons dine', and were placed on the table 'flanking' the main dishes. He specifically mentions ducks left whole and served in different dishes from the 'entrées' or 'removes', adding that 'they are also a great addition to the appearance of the table.'

Fashion also dictated where in the dinner different foods should be served. Jean Anthelme Brillat-Savarin, the French gastronome, suggested that the roast, being the highlight of the meal, should be served first of all after the soup, and all the lighter dishes should follow. Carême's menus often had the first course starting with the roast joint. To him, soup was not part of the meal, merely the prelude. However, the English did not take up the idea of the soup as merely a prelude to a meal, and certainly objected to serving the roast joint first of all, followed by the lighter dishes. Gradually the English meal of hors d'oeuvre, soup, fish, meat, and sweet evolved.

By far the most curious custom at formal dinner parties in the eighteenth and nineteenth centuries was the segregation of the sexes after the meal had been served. After the dessert, the ladies would retire to take tea, probably in the drawing room.

The gentlemen, however, would remain at table and take port, smoke cigars, and probably get drunk. Mrs Beeton had the following comments to make on the subject:

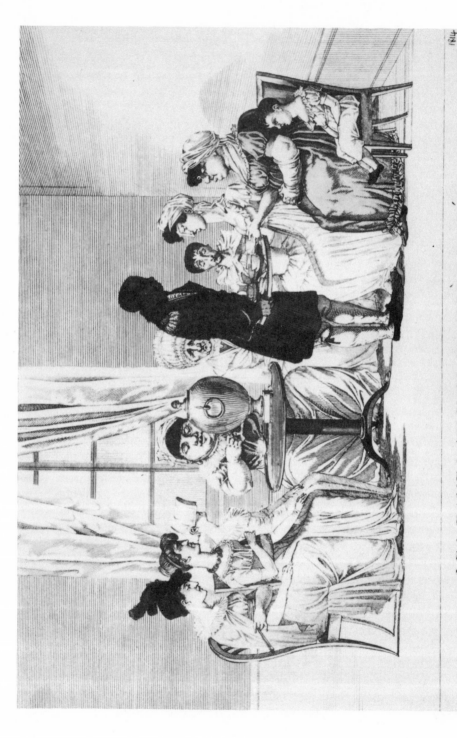

LES DAMES ANGLAISES APRÈS-DINÉ.

L'APRÈS-DINÉE DES ANGLAIS

In former times, when the bottle circulated freely amongst the guests, it was necessary for the ladies to retire earlier than they do at the present, for the gentlemen of the company soon became unfit to conduct themselves with that decorum which is essential in the presence of ladies. Delicacy of conduct towards the female sex has increased with the esteem in which they are universally held, and thus the very early withdrawal of the ladies from the dining room is to be deprecated. A lull in the conversation will seasonably indicate the moment for the ladies' departure.

Mrs Beeton was being quite polite, and did not mention one of the main reasons for the segregation of the sexes after dinner. In Regency times it was quite common for chamberpots to be kept in the dining-room sideboard, so that gentlemen who had imbibed too much liquid could quietly relieve themselves.

* * * * * * *

VI

DEATH

IN MYSTERIOUS CIRCUMSTANCES

On the 24th February, 1827 Kitchiner wrote the following letter. We do not know to whom it was addressed, but it was clearly somebody involved with the preparation of the new 1827 edition of *The Cook's Oracle*. The letter runs as follows:

> Dear Sir
>
> Since I wrote to you, I have received a very friendly letter from Mr. Cadell – liberally offering me as many Copies as I please of the Cookery – however Mr Bayliss the Printer has sent me 24 – and I think I shall not want more – : when I travel Easterly I shall call upon you & hope to hear a good account of the progress of our new Edition
>
> I am Dear Sir
> Yours sincerely
> W. Kitchiner.
> 43 Warren St.
> 24th Feb. 27.
>
> beg your acceptance of some Zest.

63

Dear Sir,

Since I wrote to you, I have received a very friendly letter from Mr Cadell – liberally offering me as many copies as I please of the Cookery – however Mr Bayliss, the printer has sent me 24 – and I think I shall not want more:- when I travel Easterly I shall call upon you and hope to hear a good account of the progress of our new edition.- I am Dear Sir, Yours sincerely,

W Kitchiner, 43 Warren Street, 24th Feb 27.

I beg your acceptance of some Zest.*

Kitchiner refers here to Mr Cadell who was the publisher, and Mr Bayliss the printer. His handwriting is freeflowing, and the letter is clearly written by a man in good health, looking forward to a journey at Easter time to see how the new edition of *The Cook's Oracle* was progressing. The last line is interesting as Dr Kitchiner has sent a consignment of his special Zest Sauce as a gift.

However, this happy and eager state of anticipation was to be suddenly changed, as on 26th February, only two days later, Dr Kitchiner and William Jerdan were entertained by their friend John Braham at 69 Baker Street. According to Jerdan, and extracts taken from *The Gentleman's Magazine* and *The Times*:

The end of poor Kitchiner's career was a melancholy one. A very agreeable evening party at Mr Braham's, redolent of charming music, was concluded by the usual petit souper, which means a rather luxurious supper. Sir John Stevenson and other musical celebrities were there, and Kitchiner was in his glory. He forgot all about his rule of retiring at eleven, and in the height of his enjoyment was above all delighted with a pet macaw, who would sit on the shoulder of our hostess, and, apparently listening to every fine movement, threw in a discord or a plaudit of its own. The mind when most disturbed or anxious, or even deeply depressed, is apt to fly into an opposite though temporary extreme, to be amused with trifles and play with idle pleasures. None present were aware that the droll attraction of the 'foreign fowl' was serving as a screen to conceal a cloud of carking care, and helped to detain the Doctor for two hours or more beyond the magic eleven.

That day he had several stomach pains and palpitations of the heart.

* Reproduction of Dr Kitchiner's letter of 24th February 1827. This letter is reproduced by kind permission of Eric Quayle.

He ordered his carriage at 8.30pm but stayed with Braham until 11.00pm. On his way home he was violently ill with heart palpitations again. On reaching home, he ascended the stairs with a hurried step, and threw himself on a sofa. Every assistance was immediately afforded but in less than an hour he expired, without consciousness and without a pang.

Yet so it was – sad lesson to humanity. We learned afterwards that, owing to domestic circumstances, he had prepared a settlement which would inflict contingencies or restrictions on the inheritance of his son, and that the following day was fixed for his signature. At nine o'clock in the morning he was dead. His departure was unobserved: he was only fifty-two years old. We could have better spared a better man; yet with all his foibles he was inoffensive and kind-hearted.*

What Jerdan is referring to here is the hatred between father and son which came to a head in 1824. Kitchiner called in Sir John Soane as arbitrator to settle the dispute, and the compromise he suggested was that William Brown Kitchiner should agree to work for two years in a business or profession of his own choice after leaving Cambridge. William Brown Kitchiner did not agree to this, and continued with his carefree lifestyle. This angered his father so much that he prepared a codicil disinheriting his son. When he died he still had the unsigned codicil in his pocket.

At the coroner's inquest on the death of Dr Kitchiner, Mr Robins, who had been Kitchiner's surgeon and friend for some years gave evidence that he suffered from a disease of the heart, and was also subject to frequent spasmodic affections, which Mr Robins thought one day might well terminate his existence. Kitchiner often declared to Mr Robins that he knew his disorder would take him off suddenly, and was in continual fear of death.

On the day in question, the 26th February, Robins had called at Kitchiner's house at about 8.00pm expecting to find him at home. As he was not there, he returned to his own house, but was later called at midnight by Kitchiner's footman, William Antiss. Both of them hastened to the Doctor's house but the patient was found to be dead. An attempt to bleed him was quite ineffectual, though the blood drawn was exceedingly dark.

*The Times, February 1827, *The Gentleman's Magazine*, May 1827 and William Jerdan's *Men I have Known*.

When William Antiss gave evidence, he stated that he came home with his master at about 11pm, and on letting him out of his carriage thought something more than common was wrong with him. They went to their apartments, and before 12.OO o'clock he was alarmed by the loud ringing of his master's bedroom bell. When he arrived at Dr Kitchiner's bedroom, the housekeeper was there, who begged him to send up some warm water and brandy, and hasten for the surgeon, as she feared the master was dying. The footman then went for Mr Robins. Kitchiner had given directions that whenever he should be taken ill, his feet might be bathed in warm water, and a little brandy administered. Mary Ann Beams, the housemaid, corroborated the evidence.

After viewing the body, the jury, under the direction of the coroner, returned a verdict 'that the deceased died by the visitation of God.'

While we can accept the likelihood of a fatal heart attack, because Robins mentions Kitchiner's past condition, we still have not accounted for such an extraordinarily convenient and timely death when the Doctor's signature was needed the next morning on the new Will which disinherited his son. The only person who would have benefited from the Doctor's sudden death would have been William Brown Kitchiner himself. There are others who share our view. The following extract comes from Eric Quayle's *Old Cook Books*:

> As the new Will remained unsigned Kitchiner's son inherited his father's entire estate. One wonders what a modern inquest might have revealed, for a faint odour of mystery surrounds Dr William Kitchiner's very convenient death.

William Brown Kitchiner would probably have known of his father's heart condition because Mr Robins, the surgeon, made house visits to see the Doctor. He was also aware of the new codicil to the Will because of his blatant refusal to earn a living for two years. If he was to inherit his father's estate under the old Will, the death had to be effected by the morning of the 27th February.

This goal was certainly achieved, and the coroner's verdict that 'the deceased died by the visitation of God' could have meant almost anything.

It is quite possible that Kitchiner was poisoned by mushrooms, at some time between the 24th February (when he seemed in high spirits) and the 26th February (the date of his death). As there is sometimes a delay of from twelve to twenty-four hours after eating certain Amanita toxins before the symptoms become apparent, suspicion would not have been aroused and they could have passed almost undetected.

The symptoms described by William Jerdan – 'stomach pains and palpitations of the heart' are the same as would be experienced by mushroom poisoning. There are two mushrooms that are deadly and are growing wild in the fields of Britain.

Amanita Phalloides (Death Cap), the most dangerous of all mushrooms, is nearly always deadly. The beginning of the symptons for phalline poisoning (Amanita Toxin) are delayed – twelve to twenty-four hours after eating, sometimes more (which will account for the suspicion of poisoning not being aroused) and they manifest themselves by burning stomach pains and intestinal disturbances. The mind is not affected until the final period, when the pulse slows down, breathing becomes difficult, the patient turns yellow and then prostration sets in followed by collapse. Death from this follows in sixty per cent of cases today, and probably death would have occurred in ninety nine per cent of cases in the 182Os.

Amanita Verna (Gill) is probably a variety of Amanita Phalloides. The symptoms are the same. These mushrooms appear in summer to late autumn, but can sometimes, on very rare occasions, appear in spring. As Kitchiner died in February, fresh mushrooms would not have been available, so if mushroom poisoning did cause his death, then it probably would have been in the form of a toxin previously prepared from fresh mushrooms, and added to a Mushroom Ketchup (or Catsup).

Kitchiner had found ways of preserving mushrooms. In *The Cook's Oracle* he gives a lengthy description of the preparation, suggesting that it can be bottled and sealed with bottle cement, so that 'it may be preserved for a long time.' He adds, 'after the mushrooms have been squeezed, dry them in the Dutch oven and make mushroom powder,' which was another older method of preservation.

William Brown Kitchiner knew of these techniques, for he published and edited his father's books right up until his own death.

Kitchiner's remains were interred in the family vault at St Clement Danes church, on March 6th, 1827. This amiable and unique man possessed the estimable virtue of never speaking ill of anyone: on the contrary, he was a great lover of conciliation, and to many he proved a valuable adviser and a firm friend. In manner he was quiet, and apparently timid. But whenever he entered upon any of his grand hobbies he was cheerful and eloquent.

Although the circumstances of his death are mysterious and sinister, Dr Kitchiner left a Will which clearly specified his wishes and his concern for the welfare of those people he considered his friends and dependants. We reproduce it here and it is well worth a close look, for it is quite extraordinary. Though his legal wife was still living at his death – no provision for her is made anywhere.

I desire to be buried in my family vault in the burial ground adjoining Saint Clement Danes Workhouse.

I give and bequeath unto my natural and reputed son William Brown Kitchiner, now a student at St John's College, Cambridge, but occasionally residing with me in Warren Street, aforesaid, all my Freehold, Copyhold and Leasehold messuages, wharfs and lands and roads with all their appurtenances whatsoever and wheresoever situate to hold such of my estates as are Freehold and Copyhold of In inheritance unto and to the use of the said William Brown Kitchiner, his heirs and assigns for ever and to hold such of my Estates as are Leasehold unto the said William Brown Kitchiner, and I recommend to my said son as soon as conveniently may be after my decease to make and execute this will.

In case my said natural and reputed son shall depart this life during my lifetime leaving no issue who shall live to attain the age of 21 years, then I give and devise all my freehold messuages, houses, wharfs and premises situate at the back of Beaufort Buildings and Fountain Court in the Strand in the County of Middlesex unto my friends Jacob William Robins of Tottenham Court Road in the said County, Surgeon, and Philip Hardwick of Russell Square in the said County, Architect.

And I give and devise my share in Copyhold Estates in Tottenham Court and in Windmill Street in the event aforesaid unto and for the use of Elizabeth Friend, Spinster, now resident in my house in Warren Street, her heirs and assigns forever and in the event aforesaid I give all my Leasehold Estates in Warren Street unto the said Elizabeth Friend.

And I give unto the said Elizabeth Friend an annuity or clear yearly sum of one hundred pounds to be paid to her quarterly during her life in like manner as the said annuity of thirty pounds is directed to be paid.

And I give unto my late footman George Thompson an annuity or clear yearly sum of thirty pounds to be paid to him quarterly during his life without any deductions.

I give unto Elizabeth Friend all the furniture that is in her bedroom and in the Drawing Room at Warren Street aforesaid.

And I give unto George Thompson a legacy of fifty pounds and the note of hand which he owes me of one hundred pounds which I lent him on his marriage.

And I give unto Thomas Henry Sheldon who was formerly apprenticed to Mr Swallow, hatter, on Saint James Street, a legacy of one hundred pounds.

And I do give unto my valued friend Edward Erskine Justin, Gent, of [undecipherable] Street, Westminster, a legacy of one hundred pounds.

And I give unto John Thurkettle my coachman a legacy of one hundred pounds.

And to my old friend Joseph Caulfield of Camden Town a legacy of one hundred pounds.

And to my cook, footman and housemaid I give a legacy to each after the rate of five pounds for each year they have been in my service.

And lastly I give and bequeath all the rent residue and remainder of my real and personal estate whatsoever and wheresoever unto my said natural and reputed son William Brown Kitchiner, his heirs, executors, administrators and assigns, and in case of his death during my life I give the same to the said Philip Hardwick.

St. Clement Danes 1827, drawing by N. Foster.

The small bequests are particularly interesting, for example the hundred pounds left to Thomas Henry Sheldon 'who was formerly apprenticed to Mr Swallow, hatter, on Saint James Street.' And 'Mr Edward Erskine Justin, Gent, of Westminster, a legacy of one hundred pounds'. Why should he have left money to two men not apparently related or beholden to him? Could it be that his disappointment with his son might have made him look elsewhere for the companionship and interest he had hoped for in William Brown, and that he had formed affectionate friendships with other young men to fill that void in his life?

Shortly after Dr Kitchiner's death, Thomas Hood penned this ode to his memory:

> *Immortal Kitchener! Thy fame*
> *Shall keep itself when time makes game*
> *Of other men's – yea, it shall keep all weathers,*
> *And thou shalt be upheld by thy pen feathers.*
>
> *Yea, by the sauce of Michael Kelly*
> *Thy name shall perish never,*
> *But be magnified for ever –*
> *By those whose eyes are bigger than their belly.*
>
> *The tender morsels on the palate melt*
> *And all the force of COOKERY is felt.*

Kitchiner would not have been very pleased by this ode. There was an error in the spelling of his name, and Thomas Hood had linked his Zest Sauce with Michael Kelly, who was a famous Irish actor.

Kitchiner's obituary notice says that a monument is to be erected to his memory in the new church of St Pancras, in whose parish he had long resided. The monument was duly completed, and takes the form of a memorial tablet fixed to the south wall of the parish church of St Pancras, Euston Road, London, where it can still be seen today. It reads as follows:

To WILLIAM KITCHINER, M.D.

Possessing a heart of unbounded kindness,
United to an intellect
Of singular acuteness, diligance and
Comprehensiveness;
Whose life was an epitome of that beautiful spirit of
Christianity which teaches us to be
"Humble, lowly, trusting in God."
He from an early period devoted himself to knowledge,
For the purpose of benevolence;
And, among various other objects embraced by his
Enlarged mind, was deeply conversant with medical Science,
Which his fortune rendered it unnecessary for him
To pursue as a profession.
An accomplished musical theorist and composer;
An improver of the telescope;
And, by his various writings, largely contributed to
Promote the happiness of his fellow-creatures.
Deeply regretted by a numerous circle of sincere Friends,
He closed his life of unaffected piety, charity and utility.
On the 27th February, 1827, aged 48 years.
To perpetuate the memory of so excellent a man,
And as merited tribute of duty, affection and respect,
This monument has been erected by his son,
William Brown Kitchiner, Esq.

Considering the caustic hate that existed between father and son, this is a surprisingly tender memorial. It is interesting to note that the son had got the age of his father wrong (for Dr Kitchiner was not 48 but 52 when he died).

Hans Busk purchased all Kitchiner's telescopes after his death, together with other scientific instruments, such as the Doctor's fine 'electrifying-machine' with all its elaborate paraphernalia, his microscope, his air-pump, and many optical appliances – presumably buying them from William Brown Kitchiner, who, though inheriting £6000 a year from his father, always seemed in need of money.

On 2 September 1828, William Brown Kitchiner married Georgina, daughter of Major Edgworth of Wilton Place, London, and they set up home in Albany, Piccadilly. Mrs Pitt Byrne describes the couple as very fashionable indeed:

> Soon after the Doctor's death, the son was bewitched into marrying a superlatively beautiful woman, whose birth, like his own, was spoken of with mystery. It would be impossible to imagine a more strikingly handsome couple – or a more prodigal mènage. 'Young Kitchiner', as he was called was an unusually handsome and elegant young man. His presence was most prepossessing, his dress bespeaking a perfect gentleman, without affectation or dandyism.

Georgina, however, was just as much a spendthrift as her husband and between them they set out on a vast unfettered spending spree, which could only have one end.

William Brown Kitchiner's study of optics at Cambridge progressed no further, and his father's books became the family business. He wanted desperately to be recognised as an author in his own right, and sent manuscripts to Hans Busk for criticism. Alas, he did not have the talent of his father, and he never published a work under his own name.

On the 30th May 1861, William Brown Kitchiner died in Ostend where debtors frequently went to escape their creditors; he was fifty-six years old. He left no Will, which usually indicates a very small personal estate, not requiring probate, or even intestacy. He had spent the vast inheritance from his father and died a debtor. The same year, 1861, the last family book *The Shilling Kitchiner* was published, the same year as the first edition of Mrs Beeton's *Book of Household Management*. An era had ended.

* * * * * *

VII

THE COOK'S ORACLE

The Cook's Oracle set a new standard in cookery books, and cookery book authors who came after Dr Kitchiner started to adopt his style. As well as his stringent rule that recipes must receive the approval of the *Committee of Taste*, a point he emphasised many times, he was one of the first writers to include weights and measures in his recipes.

For anybody wishing to recreate the Regency dishes from Kitchiner's recipes, it is most important to realise that Imperial measures were introduced by statute in 1838, twenty-one years after *The Cook's Oracle* was written, so that when a pint of liquid is quoted it is in the American measure of 16 ounces, and not our modern 20 ounces. Adjustments to the recipes must be made accordingly:

Table of Weights and Measures

To reduce our culinary operations to as exact a certainty as the nature of the processes would admit of, we have, wherever it was needed, given the quantities of each article. The weights are avoirdupois. The measure – the graduated glass of the apothecaries; this appeared the most accurate and convenient; the pint being divided into sixteen ounces, the ounce into eight drachms; a middling size teaspoon will contain about a drachm; four such teaspoons are equal to a middling size tablespoon, or half an ounce; four tablespoons to a common size wineglass.

The specific gravities of the various substances, being so extremely different, we cannot offer any auxiliary standards for the weights, which we earnestly recommend the cook to employ, if she wishes to gain credit for accuracy and uniformity in her business: these she will find it necessary to have as small as the quarter of a drachm avoirdupois, which is equal to nearly seven grains Troy.

Kitchiner was very proud of his weights and measures used in his recipes and did not like the pirating of his ideas:

> The author of a cookery book, first published in 1824, has claimed this act of industry of mine as his own original invention. The only notice I shall take of his pretensions is to say that the First Edition of *The Cook's Oracle* appeared in 1817.

He goes on to define the word 'gourmand' which nowadays means a glutton. In his time it indicated a 'gourmet' or 'epicure', which is somebody who savours every mouthful of food, rather than just eating for the sake of it.

As we have already said the welfare of staff was forever in his mind. Domestic service at this time was considered a good occupation for the lower classes. With this in mind he included a chapter in *The Cook's Oracle* for the benefit of servants. Besides being a very practical idea, this chapter started a trend. Later cookery book authors of the period copied his ideas and included a similar chapter in their books.

We find Kitchiner's ideas on how to look after a cook and servants both astute and amusing. It shows that not all employers were hard on their servants. He was a humane man and his references to 'support in Old Age' point the way to the old age pension.

The lack of refrigeration created real problems for cooks in the summer, particularly for dairy products such as butter, milk and cream. Keeping meat fresh was also difficult. When animals were killed the flesh had to be eaten fairly soon, although there were methods of preserving, such as salting and pickling. Pork had a very unsavoury reputation in the summer months, and it was partly because of this that it was considered mostly a wintertime meat.

Kitchiner has several recipes for Mutton, yet very few for Lamb, which is exactly the opposite of today. Mutton comes from ewes who have given birth, and farmers tended to wait until this stage had been reached before slaughter took place. Inevitably, mutton is fatter than lamb, though the flavour can be excellent. Mutton is seldom seen nowadays for most people like their meat younger and leaner than before. However, such is fashion that perhaps in the years to come Mutton will return to favour once again, and grace the dinner table, where it rightfully belongs.

The kitchen equipment available to Kitchiner was very simple indeed by our modern standards. There was little domestic plumbing, so he prescribes the use of 'spring water', which was delivered by cart or collected from the local pump. There were no ovens as we know them today; ovens, as such, were brick built and used mostly for pies and pastry, and the idea of cooking meat in them was quite novel. Saucepans at this time were still quite basic. They were usually made of iron, but some were in silver, or, in the French fashion of copper lined with tin. Aluminium was not extracted in its pure state until the middle of the nineteenth century, and aluminum saucepans were seen much later. The idea of stainless steel would have been considered a dream of the future. There were no food processors or mixing machines, so a mortar and pestle was used for grinding. Pastry and dough were mixed largely by hand, which was labour intensive, but with servants' wages very low, the purpose (let alone the invention) of labour saving cooking appliances was still unimportant.

In the pastry and puddings section, most of Kitchiner's recipes are of the plain and rather heavy type with lots of pies (often made with raised pie pastry), tarts, creams, rice puddings, blancmanges, and cheesecakes. These recipes clearly show what the Georgians liked to eat for their puddings. The fact that there are very few light sweets indicates that he was not only recording the recipes of the time, but showing what foods were in fashion.

There is not a single reference to choux pastry in *The Cook's Oracle*, but Francatelli mentions it in his *Modern Cook*. In his recipe for 'Petits-Choux' Francatelli adds a delightful little footnote that 'these are pronounced by English cooks as 'petty-shoes'. Clearly choux pastry was introduced into England in the middle of the nineteenth century after Kitchiner's time, when French cookery was becoming popular.

The Thames was not as polluted as it later became, and remained until the 1960s, and Thames fishing was quite an industry. Kitchiner describes Thames salmon and gives recipes for them.

In common with other writers of the early nineteenth century he uses some flowery language. The recipes are reproduced as he wrote them in 1817. Where Kitchiner's choice of words is unusual, we have added our own interpretation.

* * * * *

Included in *The Cook's Oracle* is a chapter about basic cookery methods. It deals with kitchen procedures rather than actual cooking, and gives an interesting insight into the Georgian kitchen.

Broths and Soups

The Cook must pay continual attention to the condition of her Stewpans and Soup kettles, etc – which should be examined every time they are used. The prudent Housewife will carefully examine the condition of them herself at least once a month.

We prefer the form of a STEWPAN, to the Soup-Pot, the former is more convenient to skim; the most useful size is 12 in. diameter by 6 in. deep: this we would have of silver – or Iron – or Copper lined (not plated) with Silver. Their covers also must be kept perfectly clean and well tinned, and the Stewpans not only on the inside, but about a couple of inches on the outside:– many mischiefs arise from their getting out of repair, and if not kept nicely tinned, all your good work will be in vain; the Broths and Soups will look green and dirty, taste bitter and poisonous, and will be spoiled both for the Eye and Palate, and your credit will be lost.

If a servant has the misfortune to scorch or blister the tinning of her Pan which will happen sometimes to the most careful cook, – I advise her, by all means, immediately to acquaint her employers, who will thank her for candidly mentioning an accident; and censure her deservedly if she conceal it. Scorching a pan may always be avoided by Browning your meat in the Frying pan – it is the browning of the meat that destroys the Stewpan.

Kitchiner is wrong here. The best way to make a brown casserole is to fry off your meat and vegetables in the actual cooking saucepan itself, thus retaining every delicious flavour possible, and not to fry it separately in a frying pan. This should be possible even in a copper pan lined with tin:

Take care to be properly provided with SIEVES, and TAMMY cloths, SPOONS and LADLES – make it a rule without exception, never to use them till they are well cleaned and thoroughly dried – nor any Stewpans, etc, without first washing them out with boiling water, and rubbing them well with a dry cloth and a little bran, to clean them from grease, sand, etc, or any bad smell they may have got since they were last used: never neglect this.

THE

COOK'S ORACLE;

CONTAINING

RECEIPTS FOR PLAIN COOKERY

ON THE

MOST ECONOMICAL PLAN FOR PRIVATE FAMILIES:

ALSO

THE ART OF COMPOSING THE MOST SIMPLE AND
MOST HIGHLY FINISHED

Broths, Gravies, Soups, Sauces, Store Sauces,

AND FLAVOURING ESSENCES:

PASTRY, PRESERVES, PUDDINGS, PICKLES, &c.

CONTAINING ALSO

A COMPLETE SYSTEM OF COOKERY

FOR CATHOLIC FAMILIES.

The Quantity of each Article is

ACCURATELY STATED BY WEIGHT AND MEASURE;

BEING THE RESULT OF

Actual Experiments

INSTITUTED IN THE KITCHEN OF

WILLIAM KITCHINER, M.D.

AUTHOR OF
THE ART OF INVIGORATING LIFE BY FOOD;
THE HOUSEKEEPER'S LEDGER;
THE ECONOMY OF THE EYES, AND RULES FOR CHOOSING
AND USING SPECTACLES, OPERA GLASSES, AND
TELESCOPES; OBSERVATIONS ON SINGING, &c., AND
EDITOR OF THE NATIONAL, AND
SEA SONGS OF ENGLAND.

"Miscuit utile dulci."

A NEW EDITION.

LONDON:

PRINTED FOR CADELL AND CO. EDINBURGH; SIMPKIN
AND MARSHALL, AND G. B. WHITTAKER, LONDON;
AND JOHN CUMMING, DUBLIN.

To be had of all Booksellers.

1827.

Stewpan.

Braising-pan.

Saucepan.

STEWPANS, SOUP-POTS, and PRESERVING PANS, with thick and round bottoms, (such as saucepans are made with) will wear twice as long, and are cleaned with half the trouble as those whose sides are soldered to the bottom, of which Sand and Grease get into the jointed part, and Cooks say that it is next to an impossibility to dislodge it, even if their nails are as long as Nebuchadnezzar's. The Editor [Dr Kitchiner] claims the credit of having first suggested the importance of this construction of these utensils.

Sand was used as an abrasive to clean very dirty pots; his suggestion of a rounded bottom to a saucepan was excellent.

In Kitchiner's time roasting indicated a joint cooked slowly on a spit before an open fire. What we now accept as roasting he regarded as baking, which it really is. It was still quite common for the local baker to cook the family roast.

Now begins the best description of spit-roasting either of us has ever seen. It is excellent, and very thorough:

Make up the Fire in time; let it be proportioned to the dinner to be dressed, and about three or four inches longer at each end than the thing to be roasted – or the ends of the meat cannot be done nice and brown.

The fire that is but just sufficient to receive the noble Sirloin will parch up a lighter joint. From half an hour to an hour before you begin to roast, prepare the Fire, by putting a few coals on, which will be sufficiently lighted by the time you wish to make use of your fire; – between the bars, and on the top, put small Coals, according to the bulk of the Joint, and the time the fire is required to be strong; after which, throw the cinders (wetted) at the back

Never put Meat down to a burnt up fire, if you can possibly avoid it; but should the fire become fierce, place the spit at a considerable distance, and allow a little more time.

Preserve the FAT by covering it with paper, for this purpose called 'Kitchen Paper', and tie it on with fine twine; pins and skewers can by no means be allowed, they are so many taps to let out the Gravy: besides, the paper often starts from them and catches fire, to the great injury of the meat.

If the thing to be roasted be thin and tender, the fire should be little and brisk; when you have a large joint to roast, make up a sound, strong fire, equally good, in every part of the grate, or your meat cannot be equally roasted, nor have that uniform colour which constitutes the beauty of good roasting.

Give the fire a good stirring before you lay the joint down; examine it from time to time, while the spit is going round; keep it clear at the bottom, and take care there are no smoky coals in the front, which will spoil the look and the taste of the meat, and hinder it from roasting evenly. When the joint to be roasted is thicker at one end than the other, place the spit slanting, with the thickest part nearer the fire.

Do not put the Meat too near the fire at first; – the larger the joint, the farther it must be kept from the Fire; if once it gets scorched, the outside will become hard, and acquire a disagreeable empyreumatic taste: and the fire being prevented from penetrating into it, the meat will appear done, before it is little more than half done, besides losing the pale brown colour, which is the Beauty of Roasted meat to have.

'Empyreumatic' refers here to the burnt smell imparted by the fire to the meat.

From 14 to 1O in. is the usual distance at which meat is put to the grate, when first put down; it is extremely difficult to offer anything like an accurate general rule for this, it depends so much upon the size of the fire, and that of the thing to be roasted.

As we have said earlier Kitchiner suggested an oven thermometer a long time before one existed.

Be very careful to place the DRIPPING-PAN at such a distance from the fire, as just to catch the drippings:– if it is too near, the ashes will fall into it, and spoil the Drippings (which we shall hereafter show will occasionally be found an excellent substitute for Butter or Lard). If it is too far from the fire to catch them, you will not only lose your drippings, but the Meat will be blackened, and spoiled by the foetid smoke, which will arise when the fat falls on live cinders.

The time Meat will take Roasting, will vary according to the time it has been kept, and the temperature of the weather: the same weight will be twenty minutes, or half an hour longer in Cold Weather, than it will be in warm, and if fresh killed, than if it has been kept till it is tender.

Everybody knows the advantage of Slow Boiling – SLOW ROASTING is equally important. It is difficult to give any specific

RULE FOR TIME; but if your Fire is made as before directed, your Meat Screen sufficiently large to guard what you are dressing from currents of Air, and the meat is not FROSTED, – you cannot do better than follow the old general rule of allowing rather more than a quarter of an hour to the pound; a little more or less, according to the temperature of the weather, in proportion as the piece is thick or thin, the strength of the Fire, the nearness of the Meat to it, and the frequency with which you baste it: the more it is basted, the less time it will take, as it keeps the Meat soft and mellow on the outside, and the Fire acts with more force upon it.

**BOTTLE JACK
AND WHEEL.**

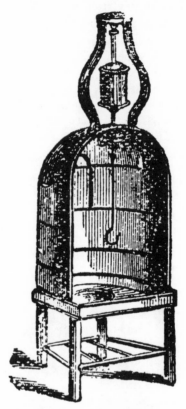

IMPROVED TIN
MEAT SCREEN.

Reckon the Time, not to the hour when Dinner is ordered, but to the moment the Roasts will be wanted. When the Joint is half done, remove the Spit and DRIPPING PAN back, and stir up your fire thoroughly, that it may burn clear and bright for the Browning: when the steam from the Meat draws towards the fire it is a sign of its being done enough; but you will be the best judge of that, from the time it has been down, the strength of the Fire you have used, and the distance your Spit has been from it. When the steam begins to arise, it is a proof that the whole joint is thoroughly saturated with heat; any unnecessary evaporation is a waste of the best nourishment of the meat.

Half an hour before your meat is done, make some GRAVY (No 326), and just before you take it up, put it nearer the fire to

BROWN it. If you wish to FROTH it, baste it, and dredge it with flour carefully; you cannot do this delicately nice without a very good light; the common fault seems to be using too much flour; the Meat should have a fine light varnish of Froth, not the appearance of being covered with a paste; those who are particular about the Froth, use Butter instead of Dripping.

Though roasting is one of the most common, and generally considered one of the most easy and simple, processes of Cookery, it requires more unremitting attention to perform it perfectly well, than it does to make most Made-dishes.

Nowadays grilled meat is very popular, and steaks in all manner of shapes and sizes are now quite familiar. In Kitchiner's time, however, this cookery method was known as broiling, a term which is still used today. However fashion has changed again. Now we like to have our steaks with good criss-cross markings on them. Not so in the Doctor's day. It must be remembered that broiling meant grilling over, or before, an open fire, anticipating the charcoal grill of today.

Double Hanging Gridiron

Broiling

Cleanliness is extremely essential in this mode of cookery.

Keep your gridiron quite clean between the bars, and bright on the top:– when it is hot, wipe it well with a linen cloth:– just before you use it, rub the bars with clean mutton suet, to prevent the Meat from being marked by the gridiron.

Take care to prepare your fire in time, so that it may burn quite clear: a brisk and clear fire is indispensable; or you cannot give your meat that browning which constitutes the perfection of this mode of cookery, and gives a relish to food it cannot receive any other way.

The Chops or slices should be from half to three quarters of an inch in thickness – if thicker, they will be done too much on the outside before the inside is done enough.

Be diligently attentive to watch the moment that anything is done; never hasten anything that is broiling, lest you make smoke and spoil it.

Let the bars of the Gridiron be all hot through, but yet not burning hot upon the surface: this is the perfect and fine condition of the Gridiron.

As the bars keep away as much heat as their breadth covers, it is absolutely necessary they should be thoroughly hot before the thing to be cooked be laid on them.

The bars of the gridirons should be made concave and terminate in a trough to catch the gravy, and keep the fat from dropping into the fire, and making a smoke, which will spoil the Broil.

UPRIGHT GRIDIRONS are the best, as they can be used at any fire, without any fear of smoke; and the gravy is preserved in the trough under them.

NB: BROILS must be brought to the table as Hot as possible.

When the fire is not clear, the business of the gridiron may be done by a Dutch oven or Bonnet.

The ordinary gridiron in those days was a frame supported on four shortish legs, one in each corner. Round bars were placed from front to back, and the broiling was done on the bars. The hanging gridiron was much more complicated, and rather like a vertical grill. The steaks or chops were hung on hooks and could be sandwiched between two sets of bars, the whole gridiron then being suspended before the fire.

Underneath the bars was a tray to collect the fat and juices. The principle is the same as used in the modern toaster.

A BOTTLE-JACK, as it is termed by the furnishing ironmongers, is a valuable instrument for roasting.

A DUTCH OVEN, is another very convenient utensil, for roasting light joints, or warming them up.

The very early kitchen ranges were just starting to appear. They were very primitive indeed.

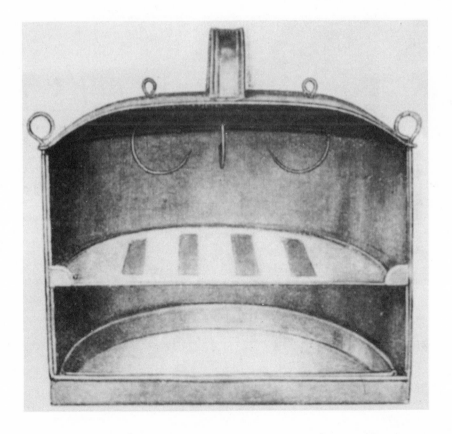

Dutch Oven

Dr William Kitchiner

VIII

RECIPES

This chapter is devoted to a selection of some of Dr Kitchiner's recipes from *The Cook's Oracle*.

SOUPS

Beef Gravy (No 186)

Called in some books Second Stock – in the French kitchen Jus de Boeuf:

Cover the bottom of a stewpan, that is well tinned and quite clean, with a slice of good Ham, or lean bacon, four or five pounds of Gravy Beef cut into half pound pieces, a Carrot, an Onion with two cloves stuck in it, and a head of celery; put a pint of Broth or water to it, cover it close, and set it over a moderate fire till the water is reduced to as little as will just save the ingredients from burning; then turn it all about, and let it brown slightly and equally all over;– then put in three quarts of boiling water; when it boils up, skim it carefully, and wipe off with a clean cloth what sticks around the edge and inside of the stewpan, that your gravy may be delicately clean and clear. Set it by the side of a fire, where it will stew gently (to keep it clear, and that it may not be reduced too much) for about four hours:– if it has not boiled too fast, there should be two quarts of good gravy; strain through a silk or tammy sieve; take very particular care to skim it well; and set it in a cool place.

As modern recipes go, the idea of an onion stuck with a clove in this recipe is unusual. There is also no thickening agent, possibly indicating a change of fashion over the years.

Game Soup (No 242)

In the game season it is easy for the cook to give her master a very good soup at very little expense, by taking all the meat off the breasts of any cold birds which have been left the preceding day, and pounding it in a mortar, and beating to pieces the legs and bones, and boiling them in some broth for an hour. Boil six turnips, mash them, and strain them through a tammis cloth with the meat that has been pounded in a mortar, strain your broth, and put a little of it at a time into the tammis, to help you to strain all of it through. Put your soup kettle near the fire, but do not let it boil; when ready to dish your dinner, have six yolks of eggs mixed with half a pint of cream, strain through a sieve, put your soup on the fire, and as it is coming to the boil, put in the eggs and stir well with a wooden spoon; do not let boil or it will curdle.

It is our opinion that Elizabeth Lister wrote this recipe. She uses the word 'tammis' which is how a professional cook would spell the word which Kitchiner frequently spells as 'tammy'. There is a full explanation of how to use a tammis at the end of the recipe for Béchamel Sauce on page 96. Elizabeth Lister is described as 'late Cook to Dr Kitchiner, Bread and Biscuit maker, No 6, Salcome Place, York Terrace, Regent's Park. Goes out to Dress Dinners on reasonable terms.' Despite the Doctor's advertisement, we do not know how successful Elizabeth Lister's freelance cooking was. We think it may have been very good, because her name appeared in every edition of *The Cook's Oracle* (and 15,000 copies were sold in the year 1822 alone). A recommendation from Dr Kitchiner was considered as a passport to prosperity.

Stock-pot.

Mock Turtle Soup (No 247)

Is the Bonne Bouche which the Officers of the Mouth of old England prepare, when they choose to rival 'les Grands Cuisiniers' of France in a 'Ragoût sans Pareil'.

This pompous introduction leads into a very English creation, Mock Turtle Soup, which, if made properly rivals the real thing, which is the 'Ragout without equal' – the real turtle soup, which is also an English invention. In the early nineteenth century, both these soups enjoyed great popularity. Both were very time-consuming to produce, but one was basically cheap, and the other very expensive.

Now follows the most authentic recipe we have seen for Mock Turtle Soup; it takes eight hours to prepare it properly. Dressing up inexpensive foods to resemble other more costly ones has been practised for centuries. Kitchiner includes recipes for mock pheasant, mock hare, mock goose, mock lamb, mock turtle, and even mock gooseberry sauce. Elizabeth Raffald writing in *The Experienced English Housekeeper* gives a recipe for Mock Brawn, while Elizabeth Moxon in *English Housewifery* gives one recipe 'To dress rabbits to look like Moor-Game', and another 'To make a white fricassee of Tripe to eat like Chickens'. Kitchiner's recipe is as follows:

Get a calf's head with the skin on, the fresher the better, take out the brains, wash the head several times in cold water, let it soak for about an hour in spring water, then lay it in a stewpan; and cover it with cold water, and half a gallon over; as it becomes warm, a great deal of scum will rise which must be immediately removed. Let it boil gently for an hour, take it up, and when almost cold, cut the head into pieces about 1½ in. by 1¼ in., and the tongue into mouthfuls, or rather make a side dish of the tongue and brains.

When the head is taken out, put in the stock meat, about 5 lb of Knuckle of Veal, and as much Beef, add to the stock all the trimmings and bones of the Head, skim it well, and then cover it close letting it boil five hours. Reserve 2 qt of this to make gravy sauces. Strain it off, and let it stand till the next morning, then take off the fat, set a large stewpan on the fire with ½ lb of good fresh butter, 12 oz of onions sliced, and 4 oz of green Sage, chop it a little and let these fry one hour, then rub in ½ lb of flour and, by degrees, add your broth, till it is the thickness of cream. Season it with ¼ lb of ground allspice and ½ oz black pepper ground very fine, salt to your taste, and the rind of one lemon peeled very thin. Let it simmer very gently for one hour and a half, then strain it through a hair sieve, but do not rub your soup through the hair sieve or it will make it grouty; if it does not run through easily, knock your wooden spoon against the side of your sieve – put it in a clean stewpan with the Head, and season it by adding to each gallon of soup ½ pt of wine, which should be Madeira, or if you wish to darken the colour of your soup, claret, and 2 tablespoonsful of Lemon juice. Let it simmer gently till the meat is tender; this may take from half an hour to an hour: take care it is not overdone; stir it frequently to prevent the meat sticking to the bottom of the stewpan, and when the meat is quite tender, the soup is ready.

A Head weighing 20 lb and 10 lb of stock meat will make 10 qt of excellent soup, besides the 2 qt you have put by for made dishes, etc.

Obs: If there is more meat on the head than you wish to put in the soup, prepare it for a Pie, and with the addition of a Calf's foot, boiled tender, it will make an excellent Ragout Pie; season it with Zest, and a little minced onion, put in half a teacupful of stock, cover it with puff paste, and bake it one hour: when the soup comes from table, if there is a deal of meat and no soup, put it into a pie-dish, season it a little, and add some little stock to it. Cover it with paste, bake it one hour, and you have a good Mock Turtle Pie.

This soup was eaten by *The Committee of Taste* with unanimous applause, and they pronounced it a very satisfactory substitute for 'the far-fetcht and dear-bought' TURTLE; which is entirely indebted for its title of 'SOVEREIGN OF SAVOURINESS' to the Rich Soup with which it is surrounded.

Many gourmets and gastrologers prefer the copy to the original and we confess that when done as it ought to be, the Mock Turtle is exceedingly interesting. Turtles become emaciated and sickly before they reach this country, in which case the Soup would be incomparably improved by leaving out the Turtle, and substituting a good Calf's Head.

Kitchiner adds that 'those who do not like the trouble of making Mock Turtle may be supplied with it ready made, in high perfection, at BIRCH'S, in Cornhill. It is not poisoned with Cayenne Pepper which the Turtle and Mock Turtle Soup of most pastry cooks and tavern cooks is, and to that degree, that it acts like a blister on the coats of the Stomach, which prevents our mentioning any other maker of this soup, which is often made with Cow Heel, or the mere scalp of the Calf's Head, instead of the Head itself.'

The Cook's Oracle is peppered with footnotes and little asides. Food in Kitchiner's London was just as subject to fashion as it is today. Here he describes the latest dish to capture the public's imagination – Mullagatawny Soup:

Mullaga-tawny signifies Pepper Water. The progress of in-experienced peripatetic Palaticians has lately been arrested by this outlandish word being pasted on the windows of our coffee-houses; it has, we believe, answered the Restaurateurs purpose, and often excited John Bull to walk in and taste – the more familiar name of curry soup. It would, perhaps, not have had sufficient of the charms of novelty to seduce him from his much loved Mock-Turtle. It is a fashionable soup, and a great favourite with our East India friends.

EGGS

Egg Whisk, for beating eggs.

Kitchiner now describes a simple egg and bacon dish, but goes into great detail. In particular look at the thickness of the streaky bacon he describes:

Eggs fried with Bacon (No 545)

Lay some pieces of fine streaked bacon (not more than a quarter of an inch thick) in a clean dish, and toast them before the fire in a cheese-toaster, turning them when the upper side is browned. First ask those who are to eat the bacon if they wish it much or little done i.e. curled and crisp, or mellow and soft. If the latter, then parboil it first.

Well cleansed dripping or lard or fresh butter are the best fat for frying eggs. Be sure the frying pan is quite clean: when the fat is hot, break two or three eggs into it: do not turn them, but while they are frying, keep pouring some of the fat over them with a spoon, and when the yolk just begins to look white, which it will in about a couple of minutes, they are enough; the white must not lose its transparency, but the yolk be seen blushing through it: if they are done nicely, they will look as white and delicate as if they had been poached. Take them up with a tin slice, drain the fat from them, trim them neatly, and send them up with the bacon round them.

SAUCES

Kitchiner describes a preparation called 'Melted Butter' which was in great use at that time. The blend of butter, flour, milk and water is known today as a panada. His recipe for 'Melted Butter' is as follows:

> Keep a pint stewpan for this purpose only. A silver saucepan is infinitely the best – you may have one big enough to melt butter for a moderate family for four to five pounds.

We have no idea why he suggests a silver saucepan here. Four or five pounds was a lot of money then.

> Cut two ounces of butter into little bits, that it may melt more easily, and mix more readily; – put it into the stewpan with a large teaspoonful (i.e. about three drachms) of Flour (some prefer Arrow Root or Potatoe Starch,) and two tablespoonsful of Milk.
>
> When thoroughly mixed – add six tablespoonsful of water; hold it over the fire and shake it round every minute, all the while the same way, till it just begins to simmer, then let it stand quietly and boil up. It should be the thickness of good cream.
>
> Obs:This is the best way of preparing Melted Butter; – Milk mixes with the butter much more easily and more intimately than

Bain-marie Pan and Pots, for
keeping sauces and entrées hot, &c.

water alone can be made to do. This is of proper thickness to be mixed at table with Flavouring Essences, Anchovy, Mushroom, etc. If made merely to pour over vegetables, add a little more milk to it.

A drachm is roughly equal to an eighth of an ounce in avoirdupois measure.

Chervil Sauce

This is the first time that Chervil, which has so long been a favourite with the sagacious French Cook, has been introduced into an English book. Its flavour is a strong concentration of the combined taste of Parsley and Fennel, but more aromatic and agreeable than either; and is an excellent sauce with boiled Poultry and Fish.

The flavour of this fine herb, so long a favourite with the French Cook, is a strong concentration of the combined taste of parsley and fennel, but more aromatic and agreeable than either, and makes an excellent sauce for boiled poultry or fish.

Egg Sauce

This is a combination of three hard boiled eggs (12 minutes cooking time, incidentally) and 1 pint of melted butter, as described above. Kitchiner suggests serving this with roasted poultry or salted fish. Egg sauce with fish is well known today, but served with roasted poultry has long since gone out of fashion.

Catsup

The early nineteenth century was an age when catsups (or catchups, or ketchups) were extremely popular, in particular mush-room catsup and anchovy catsup. However, these catsups tended to be thin essences rather than the thicker sauces of today. They were very often used as flavourings for soups and stews.

94

Dogsup

Was a catsup of double concentration and Kitchiner suggests that this method works particularly well with mushrooms. He also invented a special preparation for sealing the tops of bottles such as preserved sauces.

Tomata or Love-Apple Sauce

Tomata was an early spelling of tomato. Being red when ripe, it was supposed to have aphrodisiac qualities, and the French called it 'pommes d'amour', hence the love-apple, and the Italian name being 'pomodori' (or golden apple). The tomato plant is a member of the deadly nightshade family, and such was the prejudice against the tomato in England, that it was not accepted into cookery until the nineteenth century. As can be seen by Kitchiner's recipe it leaves much to be desired as regards taste.

> Have twelve or fifteen Tomatas, ripe and red; take off the stalk; cut them in half; squeeze them just enough to get all the water and seeds out; put them in a stewpan with a Capsicum, and two or three table-spoonsful of Beef Gravy; set them on a slow stove for an hour, or till properly melted; then rub them through a tammy into a clean stewpan, with a little white pepper and salt, and let them simmer together a few minutes.
>
> *NB:* To the above the French Cook adds an onion or Eshallot, or a little Tarragon Vinegar.

In this nineteenth century recipe, there would appear to be no thickening agent, e.g. flour. Clearly, a tomato sauce was therefore served fairly thin. Compare this with our modern tomato sauce recipe which is much thicker, made with a mirepoix (carrots, onions and celery), flour, bacon, a bouquet garni (containing rosemary, basil, thyme, parsley and marjoram), a good beef stock, garlic, and fresh tomatoes blended with tomato purée.

Béchamel
by English Cooks commonly called White Sauce (No 364)

We reproduce this Béchamel Sauce recipe in its entirety from page 304 of *The Cook's Oracle*, because it has changed so much in the 170 odd years since Dr Kitchiner wrote it.

Cut in square pieces half an inch thick, 2 lbs of lean Veal, ½ lb of lean Ham, melt in a stewpan 2 oz of Butter; when melted let the whole simmer until it is ready to catch at the Bottom (it requires great attention, as if it happen to catch at the bottom of the stewpan, it will spoil the look of your Sauce), then add to it three tablespoonsful of flour; when well mixed, add to it three pints of broth or water, pour a little at a time, that the thickening be smooth, stir it until it boil, put the stewpan on the corner of the stove to boil gently for two hours, season it with four cloves, one onion, twelve peppercorns, a blade of mace, a few mushrooms, and a fagot made of parsley, a sprig of thyme, and a bay-leaf. Let the Sauce reduce to a quart, skim the fat off, and strain it through a tammy cloth.

To make a Béchamel Sauce, add to a quart of the above, a pint of good cream, stir it until it is reduced to a good thickness; a few mushrooms give a good flavour to that Sauce; strain it through a tammy cloth.

A Tammy is a worsted cloth, sold at the oil shops, made on purpose for straining sauces: the best way of using it is for two people to twist it contrary ways: this is a better way of straining sauce than through a sieve, and refines it much more completely.

Despite all the advances in kitchen gadgetry, nothing has yet been invented which gives such a good result as the old-fashioned tammis cloth. However, it will only be found in very few establishments nowadays, for it is labour-intensive and messy to use.

As can be seen Kitchiner's Béchamel Sauce was, in fact, a Velouté Sauce, with the addition of veal and ham. Milk is not mentioned once among the ingredients! Cream was added to the Velouté, the whole being reduced and strained, thus making the Béchamel.

The following two recipes are particularly interesting, for they are both for game, and probably show the origin of the famous Cumberland Sauce which is not listed by Kitchiner, but is certainly in cookery books at the turn of the twentieth century.

Wine Sauce, for Venison or Hare

A quarter of a pint of Claret or Port Wine, the same quantity of plain unflavoured Mutton Gravy, and a tablespoonful of Currant Jelly; let it just boil up, and send it to the table in a sauce boat.

Sharp Sauce for Venison

Put into a silver, or very clean and well tinned saucepan, half a pint of the best white-wine vinegar, and a quarter of a pound of loaf-sugar pounded: set it over a fire, and let it simmer gently: skim it carefully, pour it through a fine sieve, and send it up in a basin.

Venison.

Wow-Wow Sauce (No 328)

One of Kitchiner's most famous creations, and the recipe for which he is best remembered:

Chop some parsley leaves very finely, quarter two or three pickled cucumbers, or walnuts, and divide them into small squares, and set them by ready; – put into a saucepan a bit of Butter as big as an egg; when it is melted, stir to it a tablespoon of fine Flour, and about half a pint of the Broth in which the Beef was boiled; add a tablespoonful of Vinegar, the like quantity of Mushroom Catsup, or Port Wine, or both, and a teaspoonful of made Mustard; let it simmer together till it is as thick as you wish it, put in the Parsley and Pickles to get warm, and pour it over the Beef – or rather send it up in a Sauce-tureen.

Obs: If you think the above not sufficiently piquante, add to it some Capers, or a minced Shallot, or one or two teaspoonsful of Shallot Wine, or Essence of Anchovy, or Basil, or Tarragon, etc.

Salad Mixture (No 372)

Kitchiner's own recipe for Salad Dressing:

Endeavour to have your Salad Herbs as fresh as possible; if you suspect they are not 'morning gathered' they will be much freshed by lying an hour or two in spring water; then carefully wash and pick them, and trim off all the wormeaten, slimy, cankered, dry leaves, and after washing, let them remain a while in the cullender to drain; lastly swing them gently in a clean napkin; – when properly picked and cut, arrange them in the Salad Dish, – mix the Sauce in a Soup plate, and put it into an ingredient bottle, or pour it down the side of the Salad Dish, – and don't stir it up till the mouths are ready for it.

If the herbs be young, fresh gathered, trimmed neatly, and drained dry and the Sauce-maker ponders patiently over the following directions – he cannot fail to obtain the fame of being a very accomplished Salad-dresser.

Boil a couple of Eggs for twelve minutes, and put them in a basin of cold water for a few minutes, – the Yolks must be quite cold and hard, or they will not incorporate with the ingredients. Rub them through a sieve with a wooden spoon, and mix them with a table-spoonful of Water, or fine double Cream, then add two table-spoonsful of Oil or melted butter; when these are well mixed, add by degrees, a tea-spoonful of Salt, or powdered lump Sugar, and the same of made Mustard; when these are smoothly united, add very gradually three table-spoonsful of Vinegar, rub it with the other ingredients till thoroughly incorporated with them; cut up the white of the egg, and garnish the top of the salad with it. Let the Sauce remain at the bottom of the Bowl, and do not stir up the Salad till it is to be eaten; – we recommend the eaters to be mindful of the duty of mastication, – without the due performance of which, all undressed Vegetables are troublesome company for the principal viscera, and some are even dangerously indigestible.

This is quite a good dressing. However, he suggests using water instead of cream, and melted butter instead of oil, which is very strange indeed. The 'undressed' vegetables he refers to are merely uncooked ones.

VEGETABLES

Contrary to popular belief, vegetables were very much in evidence in the early nineteenth century. Kitchiner gives sixteen ways of cooking potatoes. He also gives recipes for spinach, sprouts, Jerusalem artichokes, asparagus, seakale, cauliflower, broccoli, red beetroots, parsnips, carrots, turnips, French beans, green peas and cucumber stewed, stewed onions, and salads. There is also a recipe for the globe artichoke, a vegetable which was in vogue then, and several recipes for tomatoes. He also included a recipe for Colcannon, which was a very popular dish based on cabbage. Irish variations include Dublin Colcannon and Ulster Colcannon. The highly fashionable coleslaw of today is based on cabbage.

The recipes that Kitchiner gives for cooking vegetables are, in general, very simple. All the vegetables are boiled, even the parsnips, which he does not suggest could be better roasted.

How to remove the choke from an artichoke

FISH

More fish was eaten in proportion to meat in the nineteenth century than now; the reason for this being stronger religious feeling, with 'maigre days' much more prominent. Turbot was the most fashionable fish of the time. Kitchiner reckoned that a fine fresh thick sole was almost as good eating as a Turbot. Curiously enough, he does not mention a court-bouillon for his fish anywhere. All the fish (which would be cooked in a court-bouillon today) he boils in water, never poaches. The recipes indicate simmering, after bringing to the boil, so the word 'boiling' actually means 'poaching'.

All the fried fish is fried in lard or fat; sometimes dripping is suggested. No cooking oils are mentioned whatsoever, though olive oil was readily available. Indeed, he uses it in his salad dressing.

Fillets of Sole, Brown or White (No 147)

Take off the fillets very nicely, trim them neatly, and press them dry between a soft cloth; Egg, Crumb and Fry them, etc, as directed in (No 145), or boil them and serve them with (No 364).

Recipe 145 describes how to flour, egg and breadcrumb the fish, and then shallow-fry it. Recipe No 364 is for the Béchamel Sauce already mentioned.

Cod Boiled (No 149)

Wash and clean the fish, and rub a little salt in the inside of it: (if the weather is very cold, a large cod is the better for being kept a day): put plenty of water in your fish kettle, so that the fish may be well covered; put in a large handful of salt: and when it is dissolved,

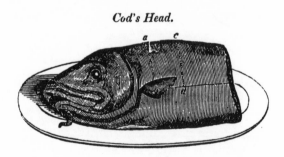

Cod's Head.

put in your fish; a very small fish will require from fifteen to twenty minutes, after the water boils, a large one about half an hour. Drain it on the fish plate; dish it with a garnish of the Roe, Chitterlings, etc, or large native oysters fried a light brown.

The sounds – the jelly parts about the jowl, the Palate, and the Tongue are esteemed exquisites by Piscivorous Epicures – whose longing eyes will keep a sharp look-out for a share of their favourite 'Bonne Bouche': the carver's reputation depends much on his equitable distribution of them.

Dr Kitchiner loved long words – 'esteemed exquisites by Piscivorous Epicures' is, indeed, very pompous. Fish-loving Epicures today still enjoy these 'tit-bits' described so carefully by him. The last line is interesting. It was common in grand households for a carver to cut up the fish, meat or game and distribute it on to the plates of the luncheon or dinner guests; much as a Sunday roast is carved today.

Fresh Sturgeon (No 152)

This recipe is included because hardly any people in Britain today have tasted the flesh of this royal fish. It was quite common in Kitchiner's time.

The best mode of dressing this is to have it cut in thin slices like

Veal Cutlets, and broiled [this means grilling today], and rubbed over with a bit of Butter and a little Pepper, and served very hot, and eaten with a squeeze of lemon juice. Great care, however, must be taken to cut off the skin before it is broiled, as the oil in the skin, if burnt, imparts a disgusting flavour to the fish. The flesh is very fine, and comes nearer to Veal, perhaps even than Turtle.

Sturgeon is frequently plentiful and reasonable in the London shops. We prefer this mode of dressing it to the more savoury one of stewing it in rich gravy, like Carp, etc, which overpowers the peculiar flavour of the fish.

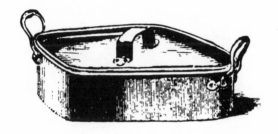

Turbot Kettle.

Whitings Fried (No 153)

Skin them, preserve the Liver, and fasten their Tails to their Mouths; dip them in egg, then in breadcrumbs, and fry them in hot lard, or split them and fry them like fillets of Soles.

A three quart stewpan, half full of fat, is the best utensil for frying whitings. They will be done enough in about five minutes – but it will sometimes require a quarter of an hour to drain the fat from them and dry them (if the fat you put them into was not hot enough), turning them now and then with a fish slice.

Obs: When whitings are scarce, the Fishmongers can skin and

103

truss young codlings, so that you can hardly tell the difference, except that a codling wears a Beard, and a Whiting does not:– this distinguishing mark is sometimes cut off; however, if you turn up his jowl, you may see the mark where the Beard was, and thus discover whether he be a real whiting, or a shaved Codling.

This is a most interesting observation. This dish Kitchiner has described is now known as a 'Curled Whiting'. It is sometimes taught to catering students in College, but they will seldom see it served in a restaurant or hotel.

Water Souchy (No 156)

Coming originally from Holland where it is known as Waterzootje, this dish is similar to the French bouillabaisse (but without the tomato, saffron, and garlic). The dish is known today as Waterzoï, and there are many different recipes for it with varying fish ingredients. It was certainly known in England for about a hundred years before Kitchiner wrote about it.

Water Souchy is made with Flounders, Whitings, Gudgeons, or Eels. These must be quite fresh, and very nicely cleaned; for what they are boiled in, is the sauce for them.

Wash, gut, and trim your fish. Cut them into handsome pieces, and put them into a stewpan with just as much water as will cover them, with some parsley or parsley roots sliced, an onion minced fine, and a little pepper and salt: (to this some cooks add scraped Horseradish and a Bay leaf); skim it carefully when it boils; when your fish is done enough (which it will be in a few minutes), send it up in a deep dish, lined with bread sippets, and some slices of butter on a plate.

Obs: Some cooks thicken the liquor the fish has been stewing in with flour and butter, and flavour it with white wine, lemon juice, Essence of Anchovy, and Catsup – and boil down two or three Flounders etc, to make a fish broth to boil the other fish in, observing that the broth cannot be good, unless the Fish are boiled too much.

More modern recipes for Waterzoï suggest a proper court-bouillon, which greatly improves the flavour of the dish. The parsley root is an essential ingredient incidentally. There is also an excellent modern variation, Chicken Waterzoï.

Findhorn Haddocks (No 157)

Let the Fish be well cleaned and laid in Salt for two hours, let the water drain from them, then wet them with the Pyroligneous acid, they may be split or not, they are then to be hung in a dry situation for a day or two, or a week or two, if you please; when broiled, they have all the flavour of the Findhorn Haddock, and will keep sweet for a long time.

The *Pyroligneous acid, applied in the same way to Beef or Mutton, gives the fine smoke flavour, and may be kept for a considerable length of time.

A Scotch way of dressing Haddocks. A Haddock is quite like a different fish in London and in Edinburgh, which arises chiefly in the way they are treated: a Haddock should never appear at table with its head and skin on. For boiling, they are all the better for lying a night in salt; of course they do not take so long to boil without the skin and require to be well skimmed to preserve the colour. After lying in salt for a night, if you hang them up for a day or two, they are very good broiled and served with cold butter. For frying, they should be split and boned very carefully, and divided into convenient pieces, if too large to halve merely; egg and crumb them, and fry in a good deal of lard; they resemble soles when dressed in this manner. There is another very delicate mode of dressing them; you split the fish, rub it well with butter, and do it before the fire in the Dutch-oven.

*Pyroligneous acid is a crude acetic acid, often called wood vinegar, which imparts a smoky flavour to food.

There is some confusion here. Kitchiner is referring to Finnan Haddock, which derives its name from the village of Findon near Aberdeen, which won fame for its smoked haddock. Findhorn is the name of a river near Forres in Moray.

Salmon or Jack Kettle.

Kitchiner gives a vivid description of the transportation of fish in the nineteenth century here:

Salmon (No 162)

The earliest that comes into season to the London market, is brought from the Severn, and begins to come into season the beginning of November, but very few so early, perhaps not above one in fifty, as many of them will not shoot their spawn till January, or after, and then continue in season till October, when they begin to get very thin and poor. The principal supply of salmon is from different parts of Scotland, packed in ice, and brought by water: if the vessels have a fair wind, they will be in London in three days; but it frequently happens that they are at sea perhaps a fortnight, when the greater part of the fish is perished, and has, for a year or two past, sold as low as twopence a pound, and up to eighteen pence per pound at the same time, owing to its different degrees of goodness. This accounts for the very low prices at which the itinerant fishmongers cry their 'delicate salmon'.

Put on a fish-kettle, with spring water enough to well cover the Salmon you are going to dress, or the Salmon will neither look nor taste well: (boil the liver in a separate saucepan). When the water boils, put in a handful of salt, take off the scum as soon as it rises, have the fish well washed, put it in and if it is thick, let it boil very gently, Salmon requires almost as much boiling as Meat, about a quarter of an hour to a pound of fish; but practice only can perfect the Cook in dressing Salmon; – a quarter of a salmon will take almost as long boiling as half a one: you must consider the thickness – not the weight – ten pounds of fine full grown Salmon will be done in an hour and a quarter.

The Thames Salmon is preferred in the London Market, and some Epicures pretend to be able to distinguish by the taste, in which reach of the River it was caught.

There are some interesting observations here. He gives 15 minutes to the pound for 'boiling' salmon, whereas 8-10 would be considered quite adequate nowadays for poaching. Again, Kitchiner suggests 'a handful of salt' added to the water.

In the late eighteenth and early nineteenth centuries there was a flourishing commercial fishery in the Thames. However, in the period from the 1850s to the 1960s, when the Thames was very badly polluted, the fishing died out. The pollution has now been largely controlled and the salmon have been reintroduced to the Thames and now occur annually in small numbers. Thames salmon, though, is still quite a rarity.

Mackarels Boiled (No 67)

This fish loses its life as soon as it leaves the Sea, and the fresher it is the better. Wash and clean them thoroughly – the fishmongers seldom do this sufficiently – put them into cold water with a handful of salt in it; let them rather simmer than boil; a small mackarel will be enough in about a quarter of an hour: when the Eye starts and the Tail splits, they are done; do not let them stand in the water a moment after; they are so delicate, that the heat of the water will break them.

This fish, in London, is rarely fresh enough to appear at table in perfection; and either the Mackarel is boiled too much or the Roe too little. The Roe of the Male Fish is soft, like the brains of a Calf – that of the Female is full of small eggs, and called hard Roe.

The best way is to open a slit opposite the middle of the roe, you can then clean it properly; this will allow the water access, and the roe will then be done as soon as the fish, which it seldom is otherwise; some sagacious gourmands insist upon it they must be taken out and boiled separately.

NB: The common notion is that Mackarel are in best condition when fullest of Roe; however the Fish at that time is only valuable for its Roe – the Meat of it has scarcely any flavour.

Mackarel generally make their appearance off Land's End about the beginning of April; and as the weather gets warm, they gradually come round the coast, and generally arrive off Brighton about May, and continue for some months, until they begin to shoot their spawn.

After they have let go their Roes, they are called shotten mackarel, and are not worth catching, the Roe, which was all that was good of them, being gone.

It is in the early season, when they have least Roe, that the flesh of this Fish is in highest perfection. There is also an after-season, when a few fine large Mackarel are taken (i.e. during the Herring season, about October,) which some piscivorous Epicures are very partial to, – these fish having had time to fatten and recover their health, are full of high flavour, and their flesh is firm and juicy: they are commonly called Silver Mackarel, from their beautiful appearance, their colour being almost as bright when boiled, as it was the moment they were caught.

It is interesting that the account Kitchiner gives of the mackerel's migration in the early nineteenth century is substantially correct today. It is curious that he suggests boiling mackerel. Though boiling was the main fish cookery method at this time, it most definitely ruins the flavour of mackerel.

Mackarel Broiled (No 169)

Clean a fine large mackarel, wipe it on a dry cloth, and cut a long slit along the back; lay it on a clean gridiron, over a very slow fire; when it is done on one side, turn it; be careful that it does not burn; send it up with Fennel Sauce (No 265); mix well together a little finely minced Fennel and Parsley, seasoned with a little Pepper and Salt, a bit of fresh Butter, and when the mackarel are ready for the table, put some of this into each fish.

Gooseberry Sauce is a long standing traditional sauce to be served with Mackerel, for gooseberries being acidic help to digest the fattiness of the mackerel.

Smelts (No 173)

Clean and dry them thoroughly on a cloth, fry them plain, or beat an egg on a plate, dip them in it, and then in very fine breadcrumbs that have been rubbed through a sieve; the smaller the fish, the finer should be the breadcrumbs. Biscuit Powder is still better. Fry them in plenty of clean lard, or drippings; as soon as the lard boils and is still, put in the fish, as soon as they are delicately browned, they are done; this will hardly take two minutes. Drain them on a large sieve placed before the fire, turning them till quite dry.

Smelts are allowed to be caught in the Thames on the first of November, and continue till May. The Thames Smelts are the best and sweetest for two reasons; they are fresher and richer than any other you can get: they catch them much more plentiful and larger in Lancashire and Norfolk, but not so good, as they are a fish which should always be eaten fresh; indeed all river FISH should be eaten fresh, except Salmon, which, unless crimped, eats better the second or third day: but all Thames fish, particularly, should be eaten very fresh; no fish eats so bad kept.

Smelts are now back in the Thames and are present in enormous numbers, possibly able to support a commercial fishery. They are best eaten in the winter – before they spawn in the Spring. In so far as there is a season, it is the same as mentioned by Kitchiner. The Lancashire smelt fishery no longer exists, although there are smelt still in the area. There is still a small fishery on the Norfolk coast.

Oysters (No 181)

The common Colchester and Faversham Oysters are brought to market on the 5th August; – The Milton, or as they are commonly called, the melting Natives do not come in till the beginning of October, continue in season till the 12th May, and approach the meridian of their perfection around Christmas.

Those who wish to enjoy this delicious restorative in its utmost perfection, must eat it the moment it is opened, with its own gravy in the under shell:– if not Eaten while absolutely alive, its flavour and spirit are lost.

The true lover of an Oyster, will have some regard for the feelings of his little favourite, and will never abandon it to the mercy of the bungling operator, – but will open it himself, and contrive to detach the Fish from the shell so dexterously, that the Oyster is hardly conscious he has been ejected from his Lodging, till he feels the teeth of the piscivorous Gourmand tickling him to death.

Milton and Faversham are now obsolete names in the oyster trade. The main source of oysters for the London market were the Kent and Essex coasts. Whitstable and Colchester lent their names to the native production. Other names such as Queensborough, Rochester and Burnham were also used in London. Each area of the Kingdom where oysters were cultivated gave its name accordingly. Most of these are now fallen out of use, as the native oyster has been largely supplanted by the so-called Portuguese oyster.*

*We are indebted to the Department of Zoology of the British Museum for this information.

110

Oysters Fried (No 183)

The largest and finest Oysters are to be chosen for this purpose; simmer them in their own liquor for a couple of minutes, take them out and lay them on a cloth to drain, beard them and then flour them, egg and bread crumb them, put them into boiling fat, and fry them to a delicate brown.

Obs: An elegant garnish for Made Dishes, Stewed Rump Steaks, boiled or fried fish, etc, but they are too dry and hard to be eaten.

This seems a strange idea – to garnish stewed rump steak with oysters that are too hard to be eaten. But such was Regency taste.

Fish Kettle.

The Milton natives may be said to be the pearl among British oysters. King John granted these fisheries to the Abbot of Faversham, in whose hands they remained till the dissolution, and they have been dredged from the earliest times by a company of fishermen, ruled, like those of Faversham, by certain ancient customs and by-laws. Murray's *Handbook*, Kent and Sussex.

Beef.

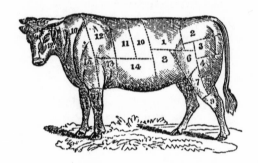

BUTCHER'S MEAT

In the nineteenth century meat was boiled more often than now. Certainly, a joint will lose less weight if boiled rather than roasted.

It is said that there are seven chances against even the most simple dish being presented to the mouth in absolute perfection; for instance a leg of mutton:

1st: The mutton must be good.
2nd: It must have been kept a good time.
3rd: It must be roasted by a good fire.
4th: It must be roasted by a good cook.
5th: Who must be in a good temper.
6th: With all this felicitous combination you must have good luck and
7th: Good appetite. The meat, and the mouths which are to eat it, must be ready for action at the same moment.

On page 363 of *The Cook's Oracle* there is a curious entry – Harrico Mutton. Kitchiner suggests that Harrico is probably a contraction of 'Haut Ragoût'. We think he was wrong, as this very old dish actually takes its name from a corruption of the French word halicot meaning a casserole or stew where the vegetable ingredients are very finely chopped. (Halicoter, to chop finely.)

Harrico Mutton (No 489)

Cut the best end of a Neck or Loin of Lamb that has been kept till tender into chops of equal thickness, one rib to each; ('les bons hommes de bouche de Paris') cut two chops to one bone, but it is more convenient to help when there is only one, trim off some of the fat, and the lower end of the chine bone and scrape it clean, and lay them in a stewpan with an ounce of butter; set it over a smart fire: if your fire is not sharp, the chops will be done before they are coloured: the intention of frying them is merely you give them a very light browning.

While the Chops are browning, peel and boil a couple of dozen of young Button Onions in about three pints of water for about 15 to 20 minutes.

Mutton.

Lamb

Lamb is a delicate and commonly considered tender meat, but those who talk of tender lamb while they are thinking of the age of the animal, forget that even a chicken must be kept a proper time after it has been killed, or it will be tough picking. Woeful experience has warned us to beware of accepting an invitation to dinner on Easter Sunday, unless commanded by a thorough bred gourmand. Our incisors, molars and principal viscera have protested against the imprudence of encountering young tough stringy mutton under the misnomen of grass lamb. The proper name for Easter grass lamb is hay mutton.

To the usual accompaniments of roasted meat, Green Mint Sauce, and a Salad are commonly added. Some cooks, about five minutes before it is done, sprinkle it with a little fresh gathered and finely minced parsley. Lamb and all young meats ought to be thoroughly done, therefore do not take lamb or veal off the spit till you see they drop white gravy.

It is very fashionable nowadays to have lamb quite pink in the middle, but, according to Kitchiner, this would not have been acceptable for a Regency or Georgian dinner party.

Grass Lamb is in season from Easter to Michaelmas. House Lamb from Christmas to Lady-Day.

Sham-Lamb. A quarter of a porkling is sometimes skinned, cut and dressed lamb-fashion, and sent up as a substitute for it. The leg and the Loin of Lamb, when little, should be roasted together, the former being lean, the latter fat, and the gravy is better preserved.

Sir-Loin of Beef

The noble sir-loin of about 15lb (if much thicker the outside will be done too much before the inside is enough), will require to be before the fire about three and a half or four hours: take care to spit it evenly, that it may not be heavier on one side than the other. Put a little clean dripping into the dripping pan and tie a sheet of paper over it to preserve the fat. Baste it well as soon as it is put down, and every quarter of an hour all the time it is roasting, till the last half hour. Then take off the paper, and make some gravy. Stir the fire and make it clear. To brown and froth it sprinkle a little salt over it, baste it with butter, dredge it with flour, let it go a few minutes longer, then take it up and put it on a dish. Garnish with hillocks of horseradish scraped as fine as possible with a very sharp knife. A Yorkshire pudding is an excellent accompaniment.

Obs: The inside of the sir-loin must never be cut hot, but reserved entire for the Hash or the Mock Hare.

The inside of the sirloin is the fillet, which is the tenderest part of the joint, and has a most delicious taste. What Kitchiner is suggesting here is to carve just the entrecôte part of the joint, which is the top section, and keep the best part for use in another dish.

Mock Hare: Cut out the fillet (i.e. the inside lean) of a sirloin of beef, leaving the fat to roast with the joint. Prepare some hare stuffing. Put this on the beef, roll it up with tape, put a skewer through it, and tie that on a spit.

Stuffing for Hare:– 2oz beef suet chopped fine, 3oz fine breadcrumbs, parsley a drachm, shallot, half a drachm, a drachm of marjoram, lemon-thyme, or winter savory, a drachm of grated lemon peel, and the same of pepper and salt. Mix these with the white and the yolk of an egg. Do not make it thin as it must be of cohesive consistence. If your stuffing is not stiff enough it will be good for nothing. Put it in the hare and sew it up. If the liver is quite sound, you may parboil it and mince it very fine, then add it to the above.

Obs: If the beef is of prime quality and has been kept till thoroughly tender and you serve with the accompaniments that usually attend roast hare, the most fastidious palate will have no reason to regret that the game season is over.

This joint is said to owe its name to King Charles the Second, who, dining upon a Loin of Beef, and being particularly pleased with it, asked the name of the joint. He said for its merit it should be knighted, and henceforth called Sir-Loin.

We both feel certain that Kitchiner would have known the true origin of the word 'sirloin', which comes from the Old French 'surloigne' or 'surlonge', meaning over and above the loin.

He also describes the Georgian and Regency fashion of fattening cattle:

In the present fashion of fattening cattle, it is more desirable to roast away the fat, than to preserve it. If the honourable Societies of Agriculturists, at the time they consulted a learned professor about the composition of manures, had consulted some competent authority on the nature of animal substances, the public might have escaped the overgrown corpulence of the animal flesh which everywhere fills the markets.

Beef Fork, for lifting large joints in the pot or saucepan.

Alamode Beef, or Veal (No 502)

In the 180 volumes on Cookery we patiently pioneered through, before we encountered the tremendous labour and expense of proving the Receipts of our predecessors, – and set about recording these results of our own Experiments, – we could not find one Receipt that approximated to any thing like an accurate description of the way in which this excellent dish is actually dressed in the best Alamode Beef Shops; – from whence, of course, it was impossible to obtain any information:– however, after all, the whole of the secret seems to be the thickening of the Beef gravy that has been very slowly stewed, and flavouring it with Bay leaves and Allspice.

Take about 11lb of the Mouse Buttock, or Clod of Beef, or a Blade Bone, or the Sticking piece, or the like weight of the Breast of Veal; cut it into pieces of three or four ounces each; put three or four ounces of Beef drippings, and mince a couple of large Onions, and put them into a large deep stewpan; as soon as it is quite hot, flour the meat, put it into the stewpan, keep stirring it with a wooden spoon; when it has been on about ten minutes dredge it with flour, and keep doing so till you have stirred in as much as you think will thicken it, then cover it with boiling water, (it will take about a gallon), adding it by degrees and stirring it together; skim it when it boils, and then put in one drachm of ground Black Pepper, two of Allspice, and two Bay leaves; set the pan by the side of the fire, or at a distance over it, and let it stew very slowly for about three hours; when you find the meat sufficiently tender, put it into a tureen and it is ready for table. It is customary to send up with it a nice Salad.

To the above many cooks add champignons; but as these are almost always decayed, and often of deleterious quality, they are better left out, – and indeed the bay leaves deserve the same prohibition.

	s	d
Onions, Pepper, Allspice, and Bay leaves		3
11 lb of Beef	3	8
	3	11

117

Kitchiner's recipe is not very specific about the quantity of flour needed. He did not have the advantage as we have now of cultivated mushrooms available fresh throughout the year. A high class hotel or restaurant 'Boeuf à la Mode' today would probably be larded with fat bacon first of all, then left to marinade in red wine for several hours, before being slowly braised in a good beef stock, with the addition of tomato purée, onions, mushrooms, a little garlic plus other aromatics. It may well be thickened towards the end of its cooking time.

We now show three recipes for Yorkshire pudding from different cookery books, starting with Dr Kitchiner's from *The Cook's Oracle*:

Yorkshire Pudding under Roast Meat, the Gipsie's way

This pudding is an especially excellent accompaniment to a Sir-Loin of Beef, Loin of Veal, or any fat and juicy joint.

1 pint of milk; 3 eggs; Six table-spoonsful of flour; 1 tea-spoonful of salt.

Make a middling stiff batter a little stiffer than you would for pancakes; beat it up well, and take care it is not lumpy; put a dish under the meat, and let the drippings drop into it till it is quite hot and well greased; then pour in the batter; – when the surface is brown and set, turn it, that both sides may be brown alike; if you wish it to cut firm, and the pudding an inch thick, it will take a good two hours at a good fire.

NB: The true Yorkshire Pudding is about half an inch thick when done; but it is the fashion in London to make them full twice that thickness.

Kitchiner's recipe contains no water. Half water and half milk makes a much lighter batter which rises, and, in our opinion, makes a better

Yorkshire pudding. Here is the second variation of the same recipe, but have a close look at the amount of milk used, as we doubt whether the pudding will rise properly:

Take four large spoonfuls of flour, and beat it up well with four eggs and a little salt. Then put to them three pints of milk, and mix them well together. Butter a dripping pan, and set it under beef, mutton or a loin of veal. When the meat is about half roasted, put in your pudding and let the fat drip on it. When it is brown on top, cut it into square pieces and turn it over: and when the underside is browned also, send it to table on a dish. W M Street, *The Frugal Housewife.*

Lastly here is the third recipe for the same dish:

Mix five spoonsful of flour with a quart of milk, and three eggs well beaten. Butter the pan. When the pudding is brown by baking under the meat, turn the other side upwards, and brown that. Set it over a chafing dish at first, and stir it some minutes. It should be made in a square pan, and cut into pieces before it comes to table. Mrs Mary Eaton, *The Cook & Housekeeper's Dictionary.*

No mention is made of salt or seasoning, and what size are the spoons for the spoonfuls? There is too little flour for the amount of milk specified, and three eggs will not make that mixture rise. In our opinion the closest to the real Yorkshire pudding of these three recipes is Dr Kitchiner's.

Sucking Pig

This was a very popular dish in Georgian times. In 1725 no fewer than 52,000 sucking pigs were eaten in the City of London. Here is Kitchiner's excellent recipe:

A sucking pig is in prime order for the spit when about three weeks old. It loses part of its goodness every hour after it is killed; if not quite fresh, no art can make the crackling crisp.

To be in perfection, it should be killed in the morning, to be eaten at dinner. It requires very careful roasting. A sucking pig, like a young child, must not be left for an instant.

The ends must have much more fire than the middle; for this purpose is contrived an iron to hang before the middle part called a pig iron. If you do not have this, use a common flat iron, or keep the fire fiercest at the two ends.

For the stuffing, take of the crumb of a stale loaf about 5oz; rub it through a cullender; mince fine a handful of sage (i.e. about 2oz), and a large onion (about 1½ oz) and mix these together with an egg, some pepper and salt and a bit of butter as big as an egg. Fill the belly of the pig with this, and sew it up. Lay it to the fire and baste it with salad oil till it is quite done; do not leave it a moment; it requires the most vigilant attendance.

Roast it at a clear brisk fire, at some distance. To gain the praise of Epicurean pig-eaters, the crackling must be nicely crisped and lightly browned without being either blistered or burnt.

A small three-weeks old pig will be enough in about an hour and a half. Before you take it from the fire, cut off the head, and part that and the body down the middle; chop the brains very fine with some boiled sage leaves, and mix them with good veal gravy, or what runs from the pig when you cut its head off. Send up a tureen of gravy besides. Currant Sauce is still a favourite with some of the Old School.

Lay your pig back to back in the dish, with one half of the head on each side, and the ears, one at each end, which you must take care to make nice and crisp or you will get scolded, and deservedly, as the silly fellow was, who bought his wife a pig with only one ear.

When you cut off the pettitoes (trotters), leave the skin long round the ends of the legs. When you first lay the pig before the fire, rub it all over with Fresh Butter or Salad Oil. Ten minutes after, if the skin looks dry, dredge it well with flour all over, and let it remain an hour, then rub it off with a soft cloth.

NB: A pig is a very troublesome subject to roast, and most persons have them baked. If you do this, then send ¼ lb of butter, and beg the baker to baste it well.

Carving instructions for a sucking pig

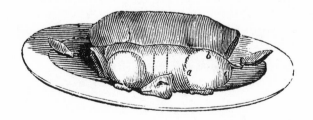

Sucking pigs arranged on a dish

GAME

The following comments on wild game are as true today as they were in Kitchiner's time:

Game and other wild animals proper for food are of very superior qualities to the tame, from the total contrast of the circumstances attending them. They have a free range of exercise in the open air, and choose their own food, the good effects of which are very evident in a short delicate texture of flesh, found only in them. Their juices and flavour are more pure, and their fat, when it is in any degree, as in venison, and some other instances, differs as much from that of our fatted animals as silver and gold from the grosser metals. The superiority of Welsh Mutton and Scotch Beef is owing to a similar cause.

Wild Ducks (No 74)

For roasting a wild duck, you must have a clear brisk fire, and a hot spit; it must be browned upon the outside, without being sodden within. To have it well frothed, and full of gravy is the nicety. Prepare the fire by stirring and raking it just before the bird is laid down, and fifteen or twenty minutes will do it in the fashionable way; but if you like it a little more done, allow it a few minutes longer; if it is too much it will lose its flavour.

Widgeons and Teal (No 75)

Are dressed exactly like the wild duck; only that less time is requisite for a widgeon, and still less for a teal.

Woodcock (No 76)

Woodcocks should not be drawn, as the trail is by the lovers of 'haut goût' considered as a bonne bouche. Truss their legs close to the body, and run an iron skewer through each thigh close to the body, and tie them on a small bird spit. Put them to roast at a clear fire; cut as many slices of bread as you have birds and toast or fry them a delicate brown. Lay them in the dripping-pan under the birds to catch the trail; baste them with butter, and froth them with

Woodcock or Snipe.

Pigeon.

flour. Lay the toast on a hot dish and the birds on the toast. Pour some good beef gravy into the dish, and send some up in a boat. Twenty or thirty minutes will roast them.

Obs: Some Epicures like this bird very much underdone and direct that a woodcock should be just introduced to the cook for her to show it the fire, then send it up to Table.

That exercise produces strength and firmness of fibre is well exemplified in the woodcock and the partridge – the former flies most, and the latter walks. The wing of the woodcock is always very tough, and that of the partridge very tender. The breast of all birds is the most juicy and nutritious part.

The 'trail' is the innards of the bird, and, with a woodcock, is considered by some to be the best part.

Larding needle, made with split ends, like a cleft stick, to receive strips of fat bacon, which by its means are grafted into the flesh of turkeys, poultry, &c.

Pigeons (No 78)

When the pigeons are ready for roasting, if you desire to stuff them, chop some green parsley very fine, the liver and a bit of butter together with a little pepper and salt, and fill the belly of each bird with it. They will be enough in about 20 or 30 minutes.

Obs: When pigeons are fresh they have their full relish; but it goes entirely off with a very little keeping; nor is it any way so well preserved as by roasting them. When they are put into a pie, they are generally baked to rags and taste more of pepper and salt than anything else.

A little melted butter may be put into the dish with them and the gravy that runs from them will mix with it into fine sauce. Pigeons are in the greatest perfection from Midsummer to Michaelmas, there is then the most plentiful and best food for them; and their finest growth is just when they are full feathered. When they are in their pen-feathers, they are flabby; when they are full grown, and have flown some time, they are tough. Game and Poultry are best when they have just done growing, i.e. as soon as Nature has perfected her work.

This was the secret of Solomon, the famous pigeon-feeder of Turnham Green, who is celebrated by the poet Gay, when he says:

> *'That Turnham Green, which dainty pigeons fed,*
> *But feeds no more, for Solomon is dead.'*

Pigeon or Lark Pie (No 13)

Truss half a dozen fine large Pigeons as for stewing, season them with Pepper and Salt: lay at the bottom of the dish a Rump Steak of about a pound weight, cut into pieces and trimmed neatly, seasoned and beat out with a chopper; on it lay the pigeons, the yolks of three Eggs boiled hard, and a gill of broth or water, and over these a layer of steaks. Wet the edge of the dish, and cover it over with Puff-paste, or the paste as directed for seasoned pies. Wash it over with Yolk of Egg, and ornament it with leaves of paste, and the feet of the Pigeons; bake it an hour and a half in a moderate heated oven: before it is sent to table make an aperture in the top, and pour in some good Gravy quite hot.

The bird's feet were often added to show what was in the pie. Another recipe of the period suggests that the feet should be left poking through a hole in the pastry; again to show what was in the pie.

Kitchiner's cooking method is very strange here. The meat appears to be raw when it is enclosed in the pastry case. After only an hour and a half in the oven it would still be very tough to eat. A much better way of making this pie would be to pre-cook the pigeons and steak pieces, then thicken the sauce, and leave it to go cold. It could then be placed in a pie dish, covered with pastry, and baked in the oven for forty-five minutes.

Trussing Needle, for trussing poultry.

The following recipe for Mincemeat is truly wonderful, and ought to be read by everyone who thinks that mincemeat comes out of little jars from supermarket shelves. This shows what real mincemeat was like, complete with actual meat.

Mince Meat (No 39)

2 lb of Beef Suet, picked and chopped fine; 2 lb of Apple, pared and cored, 3 lb of Currants, washed and picked; 1 lb of Raisins stoned and chopped fine, 1 lb of good Moist Sugar; ½ lb of Citron, cut into thin slices; 1 lb of Candied Lemon and Orange Peel, cut the same; 2 lb of ready dressed Roast Beef, free from skin and gristle, and chopped fine; two nutmegs grated; 1 oz of Salt; 1 of ground Ginger; ½ oz of Coriander seeds; ½ oz of Allspice; ½ oz of Cloves all ground fine: the juice of six Lemons and their rinds grated: ½ pt Brandy, 1 pt of sweet Wine. Mix the Suet, Apple, Currants, Meat, Plums, and Sweetmeats well together in a large pan, and strew in the spice by degrees: mix the Sugar, Lemon Juice, Wine and Brandy, and pour it to the other ingredients, and stir it well together – set it by in close covered pans in a cold place: when wanted, stir it up from the bottom, and add half a glass of brandy to the quantity you want.

NB: The same weight of Tripe is frequently substituted for the Meat, and sometimes the Yolks of Eggs boiled hard.

Obs: The lean side of a Buttock, thoroughly roasted, is generally chosen for Mince Meat.

He refers to a citron which is a special variety of highly perfumed lemon, not usually eaten as it is. It is often preserved and used in confectionery. He also mentions 'Plums'. This is very precise usage by Kitchiner. Here it refers collectively to raisins, currants and grapes.

To Make an Excellent Ragout of Cold Veal (No 152)

Either a neck, – Loin, or Fillet of Veal, will furnish this excellent Ragout, with a very little expense or trouble.

Cut the Veal into handsome cutlets; put a piece of butter or clean dripping into a frying pan; as soon as it is hot, flour and fry the veal of a light brown: take it out, and if you have no gravy ready, make some as directed in the note to (517), or put a pint of boiling water into the frying pan, give it a good boil up for a minute, and strain it into a basin while you make some thickening in the following manner: Put about an ounce of butter into a stewpan; as soon as it melts, mix with it as much flour as will dry it up; stir it over the fire for a few minutes, and gradually add it to the gravy you made in the frying pan; let them simmer together for ten minutes (till thoroughly incorporated); season it with pepper, salt a little mace, and a wineglass of mushroom catsup, or wine, strain it through a tammy to the meat; and stew very gently till the meat is thoroughly warmed. If you have any ready boiled Bacon, cut it in slices, and put it in to warm with the meat.

Veal.

PASTRY AND CAKES

When reading these recipes it is as well to remember how difficult it was to produce good pastry and cakes in the early nineteenth century. Cooking ranges were very primitive and had no real controls, so a pastry cook had to understand the foibles of his or her oven. The recipes contain no temperature guides, only a general instruction such as 'moderate', or 'hot', which, to an inexperienced cook reading the recipes for the first time would mean very little. Although there were no refrigerators, ice was available and delivered by cart in the towns. This was used in the kitchens and stored in ice boxes or 'caves' until required. At least with most kitchens being in the basement they would be cooler than the rooms above ground level.

Kitchens in large houses had a special section for pastry work away from the heat of the roasting spit. It would have had a large marble slab which always remained cool and was ideal for making pastry. However, dampness was always a problem and if flour was badly stored in sacks on the floor it could get moist. If wet flour was used in recipes it made very heavy cakes and flans, hence Kitchiner's directions to 'dry the flour before the fire'.

Despite all these difficulties, the Doctor's recipes in *The Cook's Oracle* are much as they are today. All of them indicate plain flour with eggs used as the raising agent; self-raising flour was a much later development. He does give a recipe for an Almond Sponge Cake (No 72) made with plain flour and using a large quantity of eggs. The traditional Victoria Sandwich spongecake, probably named after Queen Victoria, came later, and a recipe for it appears in the first edition of Mrs Beeton's *Book of Household Management*.

Puff Paste (No 1)

To 1¼ lb of sifted flour rub gently in with the hand ½ lb of fresh butter: mix up with ½ pt of spring water; knead it well and set it by for quarter of an hour; then roll it thin, lay on it in small pieces ¾ lb more of butter, throw on it a little flour, double it up in folds, and roll it out thin three times, and set it by for an hour in a cold place.

In using butter for puff paste, you should take the greatest care previously to work it well on the board or slab, to get out all of the water and buttermilk which very often remains in; when you have worked it well with a clean knife, dab it over with a soft cloth, and it is then ready to lay on your paste: do not make your paste over stiff before you put in your butter.

For those who do not understand making puff paste, it is by far the best way to work the butter in at two separate times – divide it in half and break the half in little bits, cover your paste all over, dredge it lightly with flour, then fold it over each side and ends, roll it out quite thin, and then put in the rest of the butter, fold it and roll again. Remember always to roll puff pastry from you. The best made paste, if not properly baked, will not do the cook any credit.

Those who use iron ovens do not always succeed in making puff paste and fruit pies, etc. Puff paste is often spoiled by baking it after fruit pies in an iron oven. This may be easily avoided by putting two or three bricks that are quite even into the oven before it is first set to get hot. This will not only prevent the syrup from boiling out of the pies, but also prevent a very disagreeable smell in the kitchen and house, and almost answer the same purpose as a brick oven.

Kitchiner describes rolling the puff pastry out thin three times. Each time it is rolled out it is called a turn. The modern method of making puff pastry is to give the pastry six turns, with half an hour between each turn in order to give the pastry time to rest.

Savoury Pie Paste (No 2):– Sift 2 lb of fine flour to 1½ lb of good salt butter, break it into small pieces, and wash it well in cold water; rub gently together the butter and flour and mix it up with the yolk of three eggs, beat together with a spoon and nearly a pint of spring water, roll it out, double it in folds three times, and it is ready.

Tart Paste for Family Pies (No 3):– Rub in with the hand ½ lb of butter into 1¼ lb of flour, mix it with ½ pt of water, and knead it well.

Sweet, or Short and Crisp Tart Paste (No 4):– To 1¼ lb of fine flour, add 10oz of fresh butter, the yolks of two eggs beat, and 3oz of sifted loaf sugar, mix up together with ½ pt of new milk, and knead it well.

NB: This crust is frequently iced.

Decorated fruit pie

Raised Pies (No 5)

The Georgians ate many different sorts of pies, and their decorated savoury ones were sometimes quite spectacular to see.

Put 2½lb of flour on the pastry board. Put on the fire, in a saucepan, ¾pt of water, and ½ lb of good lard; when the water boils, make a hole in the middle of the flour, pour in the water and lard by degrees, gently mixing the flour with it with a spoon, and when it is well mixed, then knead it with your hands till it becomes stiff; dredge a little flour to prevent it sticking to the board, or you cannot make it look smooth. Do not roll it with the rolling pin, but

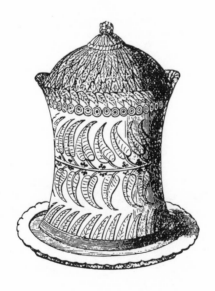

Raised pie

roll it with your hands, about the thickness of a quart pot; cut it into six pieces, leaving a little for the covers. Put one hand in the middle, and keep the other close on the outside till you have worked it either in an oval or a round shape: have your meat ready cut and seasoned with pepper and salt. If it is pork, then cut it in small slices – the Griskin (the lean part of the loin of a bacon pig) is the best for pasties: if you use mutton, cut it in very neat cutlets, and put them in the pies as you make them: roll out the covers with the rolling pin just the size of the pie, wet it round the edge, put it on the pie, and press it together with your thumb and finger, and then cut it all round with a pair of scissors quite even, and pinch them inside and out, and bake them an hour and a half.

Paste for Boiled Puddings

Pick and chop very fine ½ lb of beef suet, add to it 1¼ lb of flour and a little salt; mix it with ½ pt of milk or water, and beat it well with the rolling-pin to incorporate the suet with the flour.

Paste Jigger.

Chicken Pie (No 16)

Parboil and then cut up neatly two young chickens. Dry them and set them over a slow fire for a few minutes. Have ready some veal stuffing and lay it at the bottom of the dish. Place the chickens upon it with some pieces of dressed ham and cover it with puff paste. Bake it from an hour and a half to two hours, and when sent to table add some good gravy, well seasoned and not too thick. Duck Pie is made in like manner only substituting duck stuffing instead of the veal.

NB: The above may be put into a raised French Crust and baked; when done, take off the top and put a ragout of sweetbread to the chicken.

The following recipe was popular in the nineteenth century, but is not seen much nowadays:

Eel.

Eel Pie (No 22)

Take eels about half a pound each, skin, wash, and trim off the fin with a pair of scissors. Cut them into pieces three inches long, season them with pepper and salt, and fill your dish, leaving out the heads and tails. Add a gill of water or veal broth, cover it with savoury pie paste, rub it over with a paste brush dipped in yolk of egg, ornament it with some of the same paste, bake it an hour, and when done, make a hole in the centre and pour in the following sauce through a funnel: the trimmings boiled in half a pint of veal stock, seasoned with pepper and salt, a tablespoonful of lemon juice, and thickened with flour and water, strained through a fine sieve – add it boiling hot.

Cheesecakes have become popular in the last twenty or thirty years largely because supermarkets have included them as 'stock lines'. They are made of an infinite variety of cheese and cream toppings on a biscuit base. Compare the following luscious Regency cheesecake recipe with some of the rather ordinary modern ones:

Cheesecakes (No 40)

Put 2qt of new milk into a stewpan, set it near the fire, and stir in two tablespoonsful of rennet: let it stand till it is set. This will take about an hour; break it well with your hand, and let it remain half an hour longer, then pour off the whey, and put the curd into a cullender to drain; when quite dry, put it in a mortar, and pound it quite smooth, then add 4oz sugar, pounded and sifted; and 3oz of fresh butter. Oil it first by putting it in a little potting pot and setting it near the fire; stir it all well together: beat the yolks of four eggs in a basin with a little nutmeg grated, lemon peel and a glass of brandy: add this to the curd, with 2oz of currants, washed and picked – stir it all well together – have your tins ready lined with puff paste about ¼ in. thick, notch them all round the edge, and fill each with the curd. Bake them twenty minutes.

When you have company, and want a variety, you can make a mould of Curd and Cream, by putting the curd in a mould full of holes, instead of the cullender; let it stand for six hours, then turn it out very carefully on a dish and pour over it half a pint of good cream sweetened with loaf sugar, and a little nutmeg. What there is left, if set in a cool place, will make excellent cheesecakes the next day.

If you try this recipe, you must use fresh milk, and it must be no hotter than blood heat. Beyond this the enzyme in rennet will not work. Rennet will not work with boiled or sterilised milk.

Trifle (No 49)

This must surely be one of the most corrupted of English sweets. Trifle is a very typical Regency dish, and the following recipe is not difficult to make:

Preserving Pan, for making
jams, jellies, marmalades, &c.

Mix in a large bowl ¼ lb of sifted sugar, the juice of a Lemon, some of the peel grated fine, half a gill of Brandy, and ditto of Lisbon or Sweet Wine, and 1½ pt of good Cream; whisk the whole well and take off the froth as it rises with a skimmer, and put it on a sieve, continue to whisk it till you have enough of the whip, set it in a cold place to drain three or four hours; then lay in a deep dish six or eight sponge biscuits, ¼ lb Ratafia, 2oz of Jordan Almonds, blanched and split, some grated Nutmeg and Lemon Peel, Currant Jelly and Raspberry Jam, half a pint of Sweet Wine, and a little Brandy; when the cakes have absorbed the liquor, pour over 1pt of custard, made rather thicker than for Apple Pie, and when wanted lay on lightly plenty of the whip, and throw over a few Nonpareil Comfits.

'Nonpareil Comfits' is the old term for our modern 'hundreds and thousands', which is coloured granulated sugar used to decorate sweets and cakes.

Twelfth Cake (No 55)

2 lb of sifted flour, 2 lb of sifted loaf sugar, 2 lb of butter, 18 eggs, 4 lb of currants, ½ lb of almonds, blanched and chopped, ½ lb of citron or lemon, 1 lb of candied orange and lemon peel cut into thin slices, a large nutmeg grated, ½oz ground allspice: ground cinnamon, mace, ginger, and corianders, ¼oz of each and a gill of brandy.

Put the butter into a stewpan in a warm place and work it into a smooth cream with the hand. Mix it with the sugar and spice in a pan (or on your paste board) for some time; then break in the eggs by degrees, and beat it at least 20 minutes; stir in the brandy, and then the flour, and work it a little. Add the fruit, sweetmeats and almonds and mix all lightly together. Have ready a hoop cased with paper on a baking plate. Put in the mixture, smooth it on the top with your hand. Put the plate on another one with sawdust between, to prevent the bottom from colouring too much, and bake it in a slow oven four hours or more. When nearly cold, ice it with twelfth cake icing.

Obs: A good twelfth cake, not baked too much, and kept in a cool dry place, will retain its moisture and eat well if twelve months old.

It is unusual in modern cake recipes to find coriander as an ingredient. The inclusion of coriander in this recipe probably reflects the taste for spiciness in the nineteenth century.

Icing for Twelfth or Bride Cake (No 84)

Take 1 lb of double refined sugar, pounded and sifted through a sieve; put into a pan quite free from grease, break in the whites of six eggs, and as much powder blue as will lie on a sixpence; beat it well with a spatula for ten minutes, then squeeze in the juice of a lemon and beat till it becomes thick and transparent. Set the cake you intend to ice, in an oven or warm place for five minutes, then spread over the top and sides with the mixture as smooth as possible. If for a wedding cake only, plain ice it; if for a twelfth cake, ornament it with gum paste, or fancy articles of any description.

Rich Yeast Cake (No 60)

Sift 2½lb of Flour, with ½lb of good Loaf Sugar pounded into a pan or bowl. Make a cavity in the centre, and pour in ½pt of lukewarm milk, and a tablespoonful of thick yeast. Mix the milk and yeast with enough flour to make it as thick as cream (this is called setting a sponge). When it has lain for some time, mix it with ¾ lb of Butter oiled, 1¼lb of Currants, ½lb of Candied Lemon and Orange Peel cut fine, grated nutmeg, ground Allspice and Cinnamon, ¼oz of each. Case a hoop as stated in (No 59) and bake it in a good heated oven one hour and a half.

'Oiled' butter indicates melted butter. 'Case a hoop' refers to lining a round cake tin.

Almond Sponge Cake (No 72)

Pound in the mortar 1 lb of blanched almonds quite fine, with the whites of three eggs. Put in 1 lb of sifted Loaf Sugar, some grated Lemon Peel and the yolks of fifteen eggs. Work them well together; beat up to a solid froth the whites of twelve eggs and stir them into the other ingredients with ¼ lb of sifted dry flour: prepare a mould as in (No 67); put in the mixture and bake it an hour in a slow oven: take it carefully from the mould and set it on a sieve.

Italian Macaroons (No 70)

Take 1 lb of Valentia, or Jordan Almonds, blanched, pound them quite fine with the whites of four eggs, add 2½ lb of sifted Loaf Sugar, and rub them well together with the pestle. Put in by degrees about ten or eleven more whites, working them well as you put them in; but the best criterion to go by in trying their lightness, is to bake one or two, and if you find them heavy, put one or two more whites; put the mixture into a biscuit funnel, and lay them out on wafer paper, in pieces about the size of a small walnut, having ready about 2oz of blanched and dry Almonds cut in slips; put three or four pieces on each and bake them on wires, or a baking plate in a slow oven.

Gingerbread Nuts (No 76)

To 2 lb of sifted Flour, put 2 lbs of Treacle, ¾ lb of moist Sugar, ½ lb of Candied Orange Peel cut small, 1½oz of ground Ginger, 1oz of ground Carraways, and ¾ lb of Butter oiled. Mix all well together, and set it by some time, then roll it out in pieces about the size of a small walnut, lay them in rows on a baking plate, press them flat with the hand, and bake them in a slow oven about ten minutes.

Derby or Shortcakes (No 87)

Rub in with the hand 1 lb of Butter into 2 lb of sifted Flour; add 1 lb of Currants, 1 lb of good moist sugar, and one egg. Mix all together with ½ pt of milk, roll it out thin, and cut them into round cakes with a cutter; lay them on a clean baking plate, and put them into a middling heated oven for about five minutes.

We think five minutes is not enough for cooking these short Cakes, which are actually biscuits. Ten or fifteen minutes may well be needed

Plain Buns (No 77)

To 4 lb of sifted Flour put 1 lb of good moist Sugar. Make a cavity in the centre, and stir in 1 gill of good Yeast, 1pt of lukewarm Milk, with enough of the Flour to make it the thickness of cream, cover it over, and let it lie two hours, then melt to an oil (but not hot) 1 lb of Butter, stir it into the other ingredients with enough warm Milk to make it a soft paste; throw a little Flour over, and let them lie an hour. Have ready a baking platter rubbed over with Butter, mould with the hand the dough into buns about the size of a large egg. Lay them in rows full 3in. apart, set them in a warm place for half an hour, or till they have risen to double their size. Bake them in a hot oven of a good colour, and wash them over with a brush dipped in milk when drawn from the oven.

PUDDINGS AND OTHERS

Dr Kitchiner describes 'Puddings' here in the exact sense, that is, suet puddings, etc. At this time 'pudding' did not mean 'dessert'. Because of the difficulty with oven temperature control most of the pudding recipes are cooked by boiling. Puddings must have been baked very much by trial and error till the quirks of the cook's oven were understood. Certainly it was much easier to control the temperature when boiling something, rather than baking it.

The quality of the various articles employed in the composition of Puddings and Pies varies so much, that two puddings, made exactly according to the same receipt, will be so different one would hardly suppose they were made by the same person, – and certainly not with precisely the same quantities of the (apparently) same ingredients. Flour fresh ground – pure new milk – Fresh-laid Eggs – Fresh Butter – Fresh Suet, etc, will make a very different composition, than when kept till each article is half spoiled.

Plum Puddings, when boiled, if hung up in a cool place in the cloth they are boiled in, will keep good some months: when wanted, take them out of the cloth, and put them into a clean cloth, and as soon as warmed through – they are ready.

In composing these Receipts, the quantities of eggs, butter, etc, are considerably less than is ordered in other Cookery Books; but quite sufficient for the purpose of making the puddings light and wholesome, – we have diminished the Expense, without impoverishing the preparations, and the Rational Epicure, will be as well pleased with them – as the Rational Economist.

Milk, in its genuine state, varies considerably in the quantity of Cream it will throw up, depending on the material with which the Cow is fed. The Cow that gives the most Milk does not always produce the Most Cream, which varies fifteen or twenty per cent; this may be immediately and accurately ascertained by the Lactometer, sold by Jones, Mathematical Instrument Maker, Charing Cross, price 2s 6d.

Eggs vary considerably in size; in the following receipts we mean the full-sized Hen's Egg; if you have only Pullet's Eggs, use two for one. Break eggs one by one into a Basin, and not into the bowl together, because then, if you meet with a bad one, that will spoil all the rest:– strain them through a sieve to take out the treddles.

In old English the 'treddle', or more often 'treadle' refers to the little membrane that holds the egg yolk in position.

To preserve Eggs for twelve months, see *NB* of (No 547). This reads as follows:

Eggs may be preserved for twelve months, in a sweet and palatable state for eating in the shell, or using for Salads, by boiling them for one minute; and when wanted for use let them be boiled in the usual manner: the white may be a little tougher than a new laid egg, but the yolk will show no difference. (See Hunter's *Culina*, p257). Snow and small beer have been recommended by some Economists as admirable substitutes for Eggs:– they will no more answer this purpose than as substitutes for Sugar or Brandy.

Flour, according to that champion against adulteration Mr Accum, varies in quality as much as anything.

Butter also varies much in quality. Salt Butter may be washed from the Salt, and then it will make very good Pastry.

Lard varies extremely from the time it is kept, etc. When you purchase it, have the bladder cut, and ascertain that it be sweet and good.

Bladders were frequently used as containers for lard, and were also used as piping bags for decorating cakes and fine pastry work.

Suet Beef is the best, then Mutton and Veal:– when this is used in very hot weather, while you chop it, dredge it lightly with a little Flour.

Beef-Marrow is excellent for most of the purposes for which Suet is employed.

Drippings, especially from Beef, when very clean and nice, are frequently used for Kitchen Crusts and Pies, and for such purposes are a satisfactory substitute for Butter, Lard, etc.

Currants, previous to putting them into the Pudding, should be plumped; this is done by pouring some boiling water upon them: wash them well, and then lay them on a sieve or cloth before the fire, pick them clean from the stones:– this not only makes them look better, but cleanses them from all dirt.

Raisins, Figs, Dried Cherries, Candied Orange and Lemon Peel, Citron and Preserves of all kinds, Fresh Fruits, Gooseberries, Currants, Plums, Damsons, etc are added to Batter and Suet Puddings, or enclosed in the Crust ordered for Apple Dumplings, and make all the various Puddings called by those names.

Batter Puddings must be quite smooth and free from lumps; to insure this, first mix the Flour with a little Milk – add the remainder by degrees – and then the other ingredients.

Be sure the water boils before you put in the Pudding. Set your stewpan on a trivet over the fire, and keep it steadily boiling all the time - if set upon the fire the Pudding often burns.

Be scrupulously careful that your Pudding Cloth is perfectly sweet and clean, wash it without any soap – unless very greasy – then rinse it thoroughly in clean water after. Immediately before you use it dip it in Boiling Water, squeeze it dry, and dredge it with Flour.

If your fire is very fierce, mind and stir the Puddings every now and then, to keep them from sticking to the bottom of the saucepan; if in a Mould this care is not so much required, but keep plenty of water in the saucepan.

When Puddings are boiled in a cloth, it should be just dipped in a Basin of cold water, before you untie the Pudding Cloth, as that will prevent it from sticking; but when boiled in a Mould, if it is well buttered, they will turn out without. Custard or Bread Puddings require to stand five minutes before they are turned out. They should always be boiled in a Mould or Cups.

Keep your paste-board, Rolling-pin, Cutters, and Tins very clean – the least dust on the Tins and Cutters, or the least hard paste on the Rolling-pin, will spoil the whole of your labour.

Things used for Pastry or Cakes should not be used for any other purpose: be very careful that your Flour is dried before the fire, before you use it, for Puff Paste or Cakes; if damp, it will make it heavy.

Meat Saw, for sawing bones in parts
of meat where the chopper cannot.
be used.

He has an amusing anecdote about an old lady who loved eating puddings:

An old gentlewoman who lived almost entirely on puddings told us that it was a long time before she could get them made uniformly good, till she made the following rule – if the pudding was good, she let the cook have the remainder of it – if it was not, she gave it to her lap dog. As soon as this resolution was known by the cook, poor little Bow Wow seldom got the sweet treat after.

College Puddings (No 105)

Beat four Eggs, yolks and whites together, in a quart basin, with 2oz of Flour, half a Nutmeg, a little Ginger, and 3oz Sugar – pounded Loaf Sugar is best. Beat it to a smooth batter; then add 6oz Suet chopped fine, six of Currants well washed and picked; mix it all well together – a glass of Brandy or White Wine will improve it. These puddings are generally fried in Butter or Lard; but they are much nicer baked in an oven in patty pans: twenty minutes will bake them – if fried, fry them till they are of a nice light brown, and when fried, roll them in a little Flour. You may add 1oz Orange or Citron minced very fine; when you bake them, add one more Egg, or two spoonsful of Milk. Serve them up with White Wine Sauce.

This is an excellent example of the evolution of a recipe. Kitchiner's recipe shows the early nineteenth-century version of this dish, in 1817, with its half a nutmeg. He stipulates a batter made with flour as the base, plus the other ingredients. At this time, College Puddings were generally fried – and the baking version was just coming into fashion. By 1900 College Puddings were still being fried or baked, but they were now made with breadcrumbs and baking powder. Half way through this century, the dish had become 'College Pudding', rather than 'puddings', and the recipe shows it being baked in the oven only. The fried version has gone altogether.

Rice Puddings Baked – or Boiled (No 106)

Wash in cold water and pick very clean 6oz Rice, put it in a quart
stewpan three parts filled with cold water, set it on the fire, let it
boil five minutes – pour away the water, and put in 1qt of Milk, a
roll of Lemon Peel, and a bit of Cinnamon; let it boil gently till the
Rice is quite tender, it will take at least an hour and a quarter, be
careful to stir it every five minutes, take it off the fire, and stir in
1½oz and fresh Butter, and beat up three Eggs on a plate, a salt-
spoonful of Nutmeg, 2oz Sugar, put it into the Pudding, and stir it
till it is quite smooth – line a pie dish big enough to hold it with
Puff Paste, notch it round the edge, put in your pudding, and bake it
three quarters of an hour: this will be a nice firm pudding.

If you like it to eat more like Custard, add one more Egg, and
½pt more milk; it will be better a little thinner when boiled; one
hour will do it. If you like it in little Puddings, butter small tea-cups,
and either bake or boil them, half an hour will do either; you may
vary the Puddings by putting in Candied Lemon or Orange Peel,
minced very fine – or Dried Cherries – or three ounces of Currants,
or Raisins – or Apples minced fine.

If the Puddings are baked or boiled, serve them with White Wine
Sauce, or Butter and Sugar.

How much more interesting is Kitchiner's recipe than the rather drab
modern rice puddings we are used to. To follow this recipe, we suggest
using glace cherries in place of the dried cherries specified, and it
might be better to bake the puff pastry lining blind first of all.
Contemporary recipes say that the puff pastry should be just on the
rim of the pie dish, rather than covering the whole of the bottom of
the dish.

The Doctor does not mention which rice he is using, but it was
probably the Carolina type, short to medium grain suitable for
puddings. Even so, the cooking time he suggests does seem very long
indeed. He suggests a white wine sauce, or butter and sugar to
accompany this dish, whereas nowadays pouring cream would
probably be served.

146

Rice Snow Balls (No 108)

Wash and prick half a pound of Rice very clean, put it on in a saucepan with plenty of water; when it boils let it boil ten minutes, drain it on a sieve till quite dry, and then pare six apples, weighing 2½oz each. Divide the Rice into six parcels, in separate cloths – put one apple in each – tie it loose, and boil it one hour – serve it with Sugar and Butter, or wine sauce.

This is a variation of Apple Dumplings (No 113)

Blancmange

Boil a few minutes 1½pt of new milk, with 1oz of picked isinglass (if in summer 1¼oz will suffice), the rind of half a lemon peeled very thin, a little cinnamon, a blade of mace and 2½oz lump sugar. Blanch and pound eight or ten bitter and ½oz sweet almonds very fine, with a spoonful of rosewater, mix them up with the milk, strain it through a napkin into a basin, with half a pint of good cream. Let it stand for half an hour, pour it into another basin, leaving the sediment at the bottom, and when nearly cold fill it into moulds: when wanted, put your finger round the mould, pull out the blancmange, set it in the centre of a dish and garnish with slices of orange.

The Frugal Housewife lists no fewer than three methods of making blancmange, including a green one using spinach juice. All three methods list almonds as an essential ingredient. By the turn of the twentieth century, the familiar blancmange, as we know it today, had emerged, a pale and sad reflection of the lovely nineteenth-century confection.

Isinglass was a setting agent made from the dried bladders of fish. Now this has been replaced by a gelatine made from animal bones and tendons.

Compare Kitchiner's next recipe for Rice Blancmange with the one before:

Rice Blancmange (No 109)

Put a tea-cupful of whole Rice into the least water possible, till it almost bursts: then add ½pt of Milk or thin Cream, and boil it till it is quite a mash, stirring it all the time it is on the fire, that it may not burn: dip a shape in cold water, and do not dry it; put in the rice and let it stand until quite cold, when it will come easily out of the shape. This dish is much approved of; it is eaten with cream or custard, and preserved fruits – raspberries are best. It should be made the day before it is wanted, that it may get firm.

This Blancmange will eat much nicer, flavoured with Spices, Lemon Peel etc, and sweetened with a little Loaf Sugar, add it with the Milk, and take out the Lemon Peel before the mixture is put in to the mould.

Apple Puddings Boiled (No 112)

Chop 4oz of Beef Suet very fine, or 2oz Butter, Lard or Dripping – but the suet makes the best and lightest crust; put it on the paste board, with 8oz of Flour, and a salt-spoon of Salt, mix it well together with your hands, and then put it all of a heap, and make a hole in the middle: break one egg in it, stir it well together with your finger, and by degrees infuse as much water as will make of it a stiff paste:- roll it out two or three times with the rolling-pin, and then roll it large enough to receive thirteen ounces of Apples. It will look neater if boiled in a basin, well buttered, than when boiled in a pudding cloth well floured: boil it an hour and three quarters, – but the surest way is to stew the apples first in a stewpan, with a wineglassful of water, and then one hour will boil it. Some people like it flavoured with Cloves and Lemon Peel, and sweeten it with 2oz Sugar.

Gooseberries, Currants, and Raspberries, Cherries, Damsons, and Various Plums and Fruits, are made into Puddings with the same Crust directed for Apple Puddings.

Apple Dumplings (No 113)

Make Paste the same as for Apple Pudding, divide it into as many pieces as you want Dumplings, peel the apples and core them, then roll out your paste large enough, and put in the apples; close it all round, and tie them in pudding cloths very tight, – one hour will boil them – and when you take them up, just dip them in cold water, and put them in a cup the size of a dumpling while you untie them, and they will turn out without breaking.

It is said that George III, 'Georgie-Porgie Pudding and Pie', was, throughout his life, mystified as to how the apple got into an apple dumpling.

Suet Pudding or Dumpling (No 114)

Chop 6oz of Suet very fine, – put it into a basin with 6oz of Flour, two ounces of Bread crumbs, and a teaspoonful of Salt – stir it all well together; – beat two eggs on a plate, add to them 6 table-spoonsful of milk, put it by degrees into the basin, and stir it all well together; divide it into six dumplings, and tie them separate, previously dredging the cloth lightly with flour. Boil them one hour.

This is very good the next day fried in a little butter. The above will make a good pudding, boiled in an earthenware mould, with the addition of one more egg, a little more milk, and 2oz of Suet. Boil it two hours.

NB: The most economical way of making Suet Dumplings is to boil them without a cloth in a pot with Beef – or Mutton – no eggs are then wanted, and the dumplings are quite as light without: Roll them in flour before you put them into the pot; add six ounces of Currants, washed and picked, and you have Currant Pudding – or divided into six parts, Currant Dumplings – a little sugar will improve them.

It seems curious to have breadcrumbs in this recipe for suet dumplings, yet not to have it in the recipe for Apple Pudding.

Cottage Potatoe Pudding or Cake (No 115)

Peel, boil, and mash 2 lb Potatoes; beat them up into a smooth batter, with about ¾pt Milk, 2oz moist Sugar, and two or three beaten Eggs. Bake it about three quarters of an hour: 3oz Currants or Raisins may be added. Leave out the Milk, and add 3oz of Butter, it will make a very nice Cake.

This is, indeed, a curious dish. The combination of savoury potato with sugar and currants is most strange.

Dr Kitchiner now includes an interesting but small section on sandwiches:

Sandwiches (No 504)

Properly prepared, sandwiches are an elegant and convenient luncheon or supper, but have gone out of fashion, from the bad manner in which they are commonly made: to cut the bread neatly with a sharp knife seems to be considered the only essential, and the lining is composed of any offal odds and ends that cannot be sent to table in any other form.

Whatever is used must be carefully trimmed from every bit of skin, gristle, etc – and nothing introduced but what you are absolutely certain will be acceptable to the mouth.

Materials for making Sandwiches:–

Cold Meat or Poultry

Potted Meat or Poultry

Savoury Meat or Poultry

Potted Lobster or Shrimp

Potted Cheese

Potted or Grated Ham

Grated Tongue

Anchovy

German Sausage

Cold Pork

Hard Eggs (pounded with a little butter and cheese)

Grated Ham or Beef

Various Forcemeats

Curry Powder, Zest, Mustard, Pepper and Salt.

He also included a little section entitled 'Observations on Pickles'. He was very fond of catsups, but pickles were not his favourite fare:

> We are not fond of pickles – these sponges of vinegar are often very indigestible, especially in the crisp state in which they are most admired. The Indian fashion of pounding pickles is an excellent one. We recommend those who have any regard for their stomach, yet still wish to indulge their tongue – instead of eating pickles, which are merely vehicles for taking a certain portion of vinegar and spice, to use flavoured vinegars such as Burnet, Horseradish, Tarragon, Mint, and Cress. By comparison of these, a relish may easily be composed, exactly in harmony with the palate of the eater.
>
> The pickle made to preserve cucumbers is generally so strongly impregnated with garlick, mustard and spice, that the original flavour of the vegetable is quite overpowered; and if the eater shuts his eyes, his lingual nerves will be puzzled to inform him whether he is munching an onion or a cucumber, and nothing can be more absurd than to pickle plums, peaches, apricots, currants and grapes.

Cress Vinegar (No 397)

Dry and pound ½oz of cress seed (such as is grown in the garden with mustard) pour upon it 1qt of the best vinegar, let it steep ten days, shaking it up every day.

Obs: This is very strongly flavoured with cress, and for salads and cold meats is a great favourite with many.

Mixed Pickle – Mango or Piccalilli (No 123)

The flavouring ingredients of Indian Pickles are a compound of Curry Powder with a large proportion of mustard and garlick. The following will be found something like the real Mango Pickle, especially if the garlick be used plentifully. To each gallon of the strongest Vinegar, put 4oz of Curry Powder, the same of Flour of mustard, (some rub these together with ½ pt of salad oil), 3oz of ginger bruised, and two of Turmeric, ½ lb of shallots (when skinned and slightly baked in a Dutch oven), 2oz of garlick prepared in like manner, ¼ lb of Salt, and 2 drachms of Cayenne Pepper.

Put these ingredients into a stone jar, cover it with a bladder wetted with the pickle, and set on a trivet by the side of the fire during three days, shaking it up three times a day. It will be ready to receive Gherkins, sliced Cucumbers, sliced Onions, button Onions, Cauliflowers, Celery, Brocoli, French Beans, Nasturtiums, Capsicums, and small green Melons. The latter must be slit in the middle sufficiently to admit a marrow spoon, with which take out all the seeds. Parboil the melons in a brine that will bear an egg, dry them, and fill them with Mustard Seed and two Cloves of Garlick, and bind the Melon round with packthread.

Large Cucumbers may be prepared in like manner. Green peaches make the best imitation of the Indian Mango.

The other articles are to be separately parboiled (excepting the Capsicums) in a brine of salt and water strong enough to bear an egg, taken out and drained, and spread out and thoroughly dried in the sun, on a stove, or before a fire, for a couple of days, and then put into the Pickle. Any thing may be put into this Pickle except Red Cabbage and Walnuts. It will keep several years.

Obs: To the Indian Mango Pickle is added a considerable quantity of Mustard Seed Oil which would also be an excellent warm ingredient in our Salad Sauces.

This recipe has hardly changed in the 170 years since it was written, which would indicate the ingredients were correct. Francatelli in *The Cook's Guide and Butler's Assistant* (1862) includes a recipe for

Piccalilla and one of his ingredients is Durham Mustard. In about 1730 a certain Mrs Clements who lived in Durham, began to grind mustard seed. She passed it through several processes, keeping the secret to herself, and eventually sold her mustard all round the country, and particularly in London, where George I enjoyed it. It came to be called Durham Mustard.

Kitchiner now continues with a most unusual description of Cayenne Pepper.

Cayenne Pepper (No 404)

The Indian Cayenne is prepared in a very careless manner, and often looks as if the pods had lain till they were decayed before they were dried; this accounts for the dirty brown appearance it commonly has. If properly dried as soon as gathered, it will be of a clear red colour: to give it the complexion of that made with fresh gathered Capsicums or Chilies, some Annatto, or other Vegetable Red colouring matter, is pounded with it. When Cayenne is pounded it is mixed with a considerable portion of Salt, to prevent its flying up and hurting the eyes: this might be avoided, by grinding it in a mill, which may easily be made close enough, especially if it be passed through a second time, and then sifted through a fine sieve to produce as fine a powder as can be obtained by pounding; however our English Chilies may be pounded in a deep mortar without any danger.

Capsicums and Chilies are ripe and red, and in finest condition during September and October; they may be purchased at the Herb Shops in Covent-Garden, the former for about five, the latter for two shillings per hundred.

The flavour of the Chilies is very superior to that of the Capsicums, and will be good in proportion as they are dried as soon as possible, taking care they are not burnt.

Take away the stalks and put the pods into a cullender; set it before the fire; they will take full twelve hours to dry; then put them in a mortar, with one-fourth their weight of salt, and pound them and rub them till they are fine as possible and put them into a well-stopped bottle.

NB: We advise those who are fond of Cayenne not to think it too much trouble to make it of English Chilies. There is no other way of making sure it is genuine, and they will obtain a pepper of much finer flavour, without half the heat of the foreign.

A hundred large Chilies costing only two shillings, will produce you about 2oz of Cayenne, so it is cheap as the commonest Cayenne.

Four hundred Chilies, when the stems are taken off, weighed ½lb, and when dried produced ¼lb of Cayenne Pepper.

Essence of Cayenne (No 405)

Put ½oz Cayenne Pepper into ½pt Brandy, or Wine; let it steep for a fortnight and then pour off the clear liquor. This is nearly equal to fresh chili juice.

Obs: This is extremely convenient for the extemporary seasoning and finishing of Soups and Sauces, its flavour being instantly and equally diffused. Cayenne Pepper varies so much in strength that it is impossible to season soup any other way to the precise point of piquance.

To Make Bottle Cement

½lb of black resin, same quantity of red sealing wax, ¼oz bee's wax, melted in an earthen or iron pot; when it froths up, before all is melted and likely to boil over, stir it with a tallow candle, which will settle the froth till all is melted and fit for use. Red wax 10d per lb may be bought at Mr Dew's, Blackmore Street, Clare Market.

NB: This cement is of very great use in preserving things that you wish to keep for a long time, which without its help would soon spoil, from the clumsy and ineffectual manner the bottles are corked.

Stomachic Tincture (No 569)

Peruvian Bark, bruised, 1½ oz [Peruvian Bark is quinine based]
Orange Peel, 1oz Brandy, or Proof Spirit, 1 pt.

Let these ingredients steep for ten days, shaking the bottle every
day – let it remain quiet two days – and then decant the clear
liquor.

Dose – a teaspoonful in a wine glass of water, twice a day, when
you feel languid i.e. when the stomach is empty, about an hour
before Dinner, and in the Evening.

This agreeable Aromatic Tonic, is an effective help to concoction
– and we are under personal obligations to it, for frequently
restoring our Stomach to good temper, and procuring us good
Appetite and good Digestion.

In low nervous affections arising from a languid circulation – and
when the Stomach is in a state of debility from age, intemperance,
or other causes, this is a most acceptable restorative.

NB: Tea made with dried and bruised SEVILLE ORANGE
PEEL, in the same way as common Tea, and drank with Milk and
Sugar, has been taken by nervous and dyspeptic persons with great
benefit.

Sucking a bit of dried Orange Peel about an hour before dinner,
when the stomach is empty, is very grateful and strengthening to it.

The following recipe is most interesting. Few people would nowadays
be able to reproduce this recipe at home – fewer still legally. Opium
was on general sale, as nineteenth-century laws were much more lax.
Consequently opium addiction was quite high.

Paregoric [Soothing] Elixir (No 570)

A drachm of purified Opium; Same of flowers of Benjamin; Same of Oil of Aniseed; Camphor, two scruples [a scruple is a unit of weight equalling 20 grains, or ½ drachm.]

Steep all in 1pt of Brandy, or Proof Spirit: let it stand ten days, occasionally shaking it up. Strain.

A teaspoonful in half a pint of White Wine Whey is an agreeable and effectual medicine for Coughs and Colds.

It is also excellent for Children who have the Hooping Cough, in doses of from five to twenty drops in a little water, or on a little bit of sugar.

Martin's Bill in Operation was particularly clever. Richard Martin (1754-1834) was known as 'Humanity Martin' because of his concern for animals. In spite of opposition from Canning and Sir Robert Peel he succeeded in carrying into law an act 'to prevent the cruel and improper treatment of cattle' and 'the first modern enactment in Great Britain for protecting the rights of animals'. It received royal assent on 22nd July, 1822, and was amended in 1835. Not content with this, he embarked on a witch hunt in London bringing before the magistrates everyone who he thought contravened his Act. He was one of the founder members of the Royal Society for the Prevention of Cruelty to Animals in 1824, and later declined a peerage. In the centre of the cartoon we see Dr Kitchiner with two friends eating 'live animals' – in other words, oysters, one of his favourite delicacies. On the left Humanity Martin is entering the door with an officer of the Law ready to arrest the three diners.

IX

FINALE

Dr Kitchiner's writings show how advanced his ideas were. Then, as now, part of the price of fame was to be the butt of satire and ridicule, and he did not escape from certain scurrilous journalists. Here is part of such an attack upon his integrity. It comes from the August 1824 edition of *John Bull*, a magazine which specialised in indiscriminate ridicule of outstanding people. Only the very famous were ridiculed in this way – so that in itself was an admission of his greatness:

> We are half sorry for having announced Dr Kitchiner as the second of this our highly popular series, after the little opium eater. For though undoubtedly the Doctor has humbug about him, yet he, by no means deserves to be ranked with so superb a specimen of it, with such a mass of humbugging pure as little Quincey.*
>
> Enough however of this – having thus recommended the kicking out of Quincey, let us turn to the knight of the knife and fork. Against him, as we have already mentioned, our charges are of a far less aggravated nature. But we nevertheless say that one of the primest features of quackery is exhibited most notoriously in his person – we mean the variety and the discrepancy of the subjects to which he turns his pen. To him the music of the spheres is as familiar as that of the bagpipe, and he looks with equal eye, as Lord of all, on the productions of Cullen or the cullender.
>
> It is principally on account of this aiming to being a walking

*The first subject in the series was Thomas de Quincey.

159

encyclopaedia that we have placed him in the seats of humbug. Like Dryden's Zimri, he is everything by starts and nothing long. Hence, with all his bustle and pretension, there is not a book of his but is infested with most outrageous quackery. His peptic Precepts are humbug from beginning to end. There is nothing worth reading in them that has not been stolen in the most barefaced manner, from a thousand unacknowledged sources. And yet he has the face to puff it off as original. In the same way he informs us that there is not a receipt in his *Cook's Oracle* which he has not tried and submitted to the opinion of a Committee of Taste! Now, this is exactly what one of that polite nation the Houyhnhnms would call 'saying the thing which is not.' Turn up Kitchiner by chance – there he is page 224: 'Put half-a-pint of oatmeal into a porringer with a little salt, if there be not enough in the broth – of which add as much as will mix it to the consistence of hasty-pudding, or a little thicker – lastly take a little of the fat that SWIMS ON THE BROTH, and put it on the crowdie – and eat it in the same way as hasty pudding.' Gods of Gastronomy! here is a dose for a horse! And Doctor Kitchiner pretends that he actually ate of that dish and submitted it to a Committee of Taste! TASTE! Foh!

Again does he think anybody with a head on his shoulders will believe him, when he tells us of his having eaten skate fried in dripping – or ox-cheek dressed with two whole onions, two cloves of garlick, two bay leaves, etc – or a fat pudding, a compound of grease, or extract of vermin under the name of soy, or a hundred other similar things. No! No! Doctor we shall not swallow either your dishes or your assertions.

John Bull took this recipe out of context. It comes in a section marked Scotch Soups in *The Cook's Oracle*, and the actual recipe is for Scotch Brose (No 205). It starts with the following introduction:

'This favourite Scotch dish is generally made with the liquor meat has been boiled in', and continues as printed in *John Bull*. The 'fat that swims on the broth' refers to the practice in some kitchens in Kitchiner's day whereby a stock pot was left to cool so that fat collected at the top of it. The fat was then clarified, that is, boiled up with water to remove the impurities and some chefs said that the fat produced by this method had more flavour than dripping. A 'crowdie' is a Scottish word embracing all dishes of a porridge nature. His recipe closes with the following observation: 'This Scotsman's dish is easily prepared, at very little expense, and is pleasant tasted and nutritious.' So we think he not only made the dish, but tasted it as well.

The skate fried in dripping was first dipped in egg and breadcrumbs which is not only very acceptable, but a very good dish, and the ox-cheek is also very pleasant. This was unfair criticism from *John Bull* which continued its attack on Kitchiner by suggesting that a wealthy man should not soil his hands by working as a cook. How else could he have written such an excellent cookery book! The article continues:

> This then is quackery of an unmitigated kind. We own, besides, that it does strike us as something infinitely disgusting, to see an elderly gentleman of a liberal profession and an ample fortune, stooping to study cookery as a working cook.
>
> Kitchiner has lately succeeded in getting up a club of writers of which he is the great critic – the Magnus Apollo – and from every one of the fraternity he receives the tribute of a puff. Of this club, if it be worth it, we shall 'ere long give a very sufficient analysis: but it is probable that it is not worth the paper which such an exposé would cost.

The reference to a club of writers started by Kitchiner is the only one we have seen. His friend the journalist William Jerdan does not mention it in his writings, so we have no further information on it. *John Bull* continues:

> Kitchiner has lately made his appearance with a book on spectacles – a barefaced reprint of a former work of the same kind, which yet is most heroically puffed off in the second number of the Universal Review. The article, of course, was written either by himself or from his dictation, and, it informs us that this bookselling speculation is a result of the 'benevolent ingenuity which marks the spirit of the author'. Benevolent fig-end! The wine our friend Kitchiner drinks is made of grapes.It is profits of the book – partly by a scheme recommended in it, of opening a depot for selling spectacles to the poor, at a moderate premium - which, of course, is intended as a job. We shall, however, believe in his benevolence if he devotes one year's profits of *The Cook's Oracle* to the design – on the same day we shall cheerfully consecrate a similar proportion of the profits of our Magazine.

John Bull was quite correct. On page 128 of *The Cook's Oracle* Kitchiner was selling his glasses in his cookery book:

> The best glasses, set in single-jointed steel frames, may be purchased wholesale, at the rate of eighteen shillings per dozen pairs; thus for

the small sum of eighteen pence, the benevolent may enjoy the gratifying reflection of giving an industrious workman the power of long continuing his labour with undimished ability, and of earning a subsistence till extreme old age. In no way can so much good be done with so little money.

Qui Visum Vitam dat.

See *The Economy of the Eyes* by the author of this work, 1826.

One word as to his name, and we have done. So complete an illustration of the prophetic spirit never was known. Tom Paine, when he sneered at the adaption of the name of Phaleg to the great occurrence which took place in the days of that patriarch, could not have anticipated that he had a contemporary (Kitchiner is about sixty), whose future occupation was distinctly shadowed forth in his name. On which subject we can give our readers a

SONNET TO CONCLUDE

Knight of the kitchen – telescopic cook –
Medical poet – pudding – building bard –
Swallower of dripping – gulper down of lard –

Equally great in Beaufort and in book –
With a prophetic eye that seer did look
Into fate's records when he gave thy name
By which you float along the stream of Fame

As floats the horse-dung down the gurgling brook,
He saw thee destined for the boiler's side,
With beef and mutton endless war to wage;
Had he looked further, he perhaps had spied

Thee scribbling, ever scribbling page by page,
Then on thy head his hand he'd have applied,
And said, this child will be a HUMBUG OF THE AGE.

The information for this article on Kitchiner had been supplied by one of the Doctor's own *Committee of Taste* dinner guests, Theodore Hook. Sir Walter Scott, recognising that Hook had a wonderful gift for acerbic wit and was the 'prince of lampooners', recommended that he should become editor of *John Bull* in 1820. Hook took the post (remaining anonymous) and made the facetious and scurrilous magazine both profitable and popular. Hook failed to discover the Doctor's pretence of having been to Eton and also being an MD of Glasgow. He missed a trick there. Kitchiner must have been hurt at being betrayed in this way, although by the standards of the time the attack was not particularly vicious.

The Doctor admitted that he had read over two hundred and fifty volumes on cookery before he produced his own bestseller; and he certainly did 'pillage' everybody else's work, so *John Bull* was justified in that accusation, but so did many other contemporary Regency and Victorian writers.

We would have loved to have met Dr Kitchiner, as there would have been so many questions to ask him. We would have loved to have told him how many of his suggestions and ideas have been realised. Above all, we would have enjoyed an invitation to some of his *Committee of Taste* dinners, perhaps with Sir Joseph Banks, Braham, Charles Kemble, Dr Haslam, and William Jerdan as the other guests. And, perhaps, have a private dinner with the Prince Regent and Dr Kitchiner himself.

The last page of *The Cook's Oracle* carries Dr Kitchiner's message to all those who have read his book - they will surely become good cooks:

FAREWELL TO THE READER

We have now made, in one design,
The Utile and Dulce join,
And taught the poor and men of wealth,
To reconcile their taste to health,
Restrain each forward appetite,
To dine with prudence and delight,
And careful all our rules to follow,
To masticate before they swallow.
Tis thus Hygeia guides our pen,
To warn the greedy sons of men,

To moderate their wine and meat,
and 'eat to live, not live to eat.
For the rash palate oft bestows
Arthritic lectures on the toes!
The stomach void of wind and bile,
Shall praise our monitory style,
And as he cannot speak, enlist
Himself as your ventriloquist –
The Head, now clear from pain and vapour,
Shall order out his ink and paper;
And dictate praises on these rules,
To govern gourmandizing fools.
The legs, now fearless of the gout
As ready messengers turn out.
To spread our volume far and near.
Active in gratitude sincere.
While thus the body, strong and sound,
Our constant advocate is found,
And pointing to receipts delicious,
Exclaims 'who reads our new Apicius,
If he has brains may keep them cool,
If a sound stomach and no fool,
May keep it so unclogged by food
Indigestion's sickly brood,
His hunger, though oppressive, ease,
His palate,though capricious, please,
And if with care he reads our book,
In theory may become a cook;
Learn the delights good rules procure us
When appetite by reasons aw'd,
Zeno alike and Epicurus
Pleasures combined with health applaud,
He who is stomach's master, he
The noblest empire then may boast,
And at whatever feast he be,
That man alone 'shall rule the roast.'

Aitch Bone of Beef.

Calf's Head.

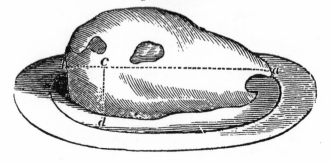

GLOSSARY

Baking Plate The old term for a baking sheet

Bottlejack A type of very primitive oven with a hook on the inside for hanging food such as meat so it could be placed in front of a fire and roasted without using a spit

Colcannon 'Cole' or 'Cale' in a dish indicates cabbage

Court A liquid used for poaching fish. It comprises *Bouillon* water, a little vinegar, some onion slices, bay leaf and parsley stalks

To Crimp To make a gash or incision in the side of a large fish before rigor mortis sets in. This makes the fish firmer

To dress To cook

Dutch oven A metal container open on one side placed before a fire used for cooking small joints, or warming large ones

To flay To skin, as to remove the rind from pork

To froth When a spit-roasted joint was almost cooked, a mixture of flour and salt was sprinkled on the outside of the meat, which then 'frothed' as the joint finished cooking

Gridiron A vertical grill used to cook food by placing before the fire

Griskin A loin of bacon often used as a roasting joint

Hair sieve A sieve of extremely fine mesh used for separating very small particles from a liquid

Isinglass A setting agent made from the died bladder of some fish. It is now replaced by gelatine obtained from bones and tendons

Kit A kit is a circular wooden vessel with hooped staves frequently used for containing pickling foods

Loaf sugar This was sugar produced in the shape of a conical loaf. You would break pieces off it as required. It has become the cube sugar which is still available today

Marmalade Fruit stewed to a pulp with sugar

Plums A collective name for grapes, sultanas, raisins as well as plums themselves

Rennet Rennet contains an enzyme that coagulates milk. It is used in making junket, cheese production and various other similar processes

Scurvy grass This is a perennial herb (Cochlearis Officinalis) which grows near the sea. It has a fleshy root stock, spoon shaped leaves, and white flowers. It was thought to be a cure for scurvy, so was introduced into the mariners' diet aboard ship

Sippets The English term for today's popular croutons – little fried cubes of bread often served with soups

Sounds The jelly parts about the jowl, the palate, and the tongue of fish

Tammis A cloth used to strain sauces or soups. The item to be strained would be placed in the tammis which would be wrung out, thus extracting all the liquid, the solid element remaining

Trail The entrails of game birds such as the woodcock, much prized by gourmets

Vermicelli A type of pasta not unlike spaghetti, but very much thinner

METRIC CONVERSION TABLE

In Dr Kitchiner's day 16 fl oz = 1 pint = 400ml

8 fl oz = ½ pt = 200ml

4 fl oz = ¼ pt = 100ml

1 fl oz = 25ml

1oz = 30g

2oz = 55g

4oz = ¼ lb = 110g

8oz = ½ lb = 225g

12oz = ¾ lb = 340g

16oz = 1 lb = 450g

12d (pennies) = 1s (shilling) 20s = £1

Where money is mentioned in the text no attempt has been made to update the value into present-day terms which are constantly changing.

SELECT BIBLIOGRAPHY

Acton, Eliza, *Modern Cookery*, 1845
Acton, Eliza, *The English Bread Book*, 1857, reprinted 1990
Ayrton, Elizabeth, *The Cookery of England*, 1974
Beeton, Isabella, *Book of Household Management*,
  1861, 1869, 1906, 1960
Boswell, James, *The Life of Samuel Johnson LLD*, 1791
Burton, Elizabeth, *The Early Victorians at Home*, 1972
Dickens, Charles, *Barnaby Rudge*
Eaton, Mary, *The Cook and Housekeeper's Dictionary*, 1822
Francatelli, Charles Elme, *Modern Cook*, 1845
Francatelli, Charles Elme, *Cook's Guide and Butler's Assistant*, 1861
Francatelli, Charles Elme, *The Royal English and Foreign
  Confectioner*, 1862
Hartley, Dorothy, *Food in England*, 1954
Hood, Thomas, *Whims and Oddities*, 1826
Hyde, Montgomery, *Mr and Mrs Beeton*, 1951
Jerdan, William, *Men I have known*, 1866
John Bull, 1799, 1824, 1827
Kitchiner MD, Dr William, *The Cook's Oracle*, 1817
Kitchiner MD, Dr William, *The Housekeeper's Oracle*, 1829
Kitchiner MD, Dr William, *The Traveller's Oracle*, 1827
Kitchiner MD, Dr William, unpublished manuscript in his
  possession, 1810
Mayhew, Henry, *London's Underworld*, 1862
Oxford, Arnold Whitaker, *English Cookery Books to 1850*, 1913
  (1979 edition)
Pitt Byrne, *Social Hours with Celebrities*, 1898
Quayle, Eric, *Old Cook Books*, 1978
Raffald, Elizabeth, *The Experienced English Housekeeper*, 1834
Ritchman, Francis, *Eighteenth Century Studies*, 1881
Rundle, Maria, *A New System of Cookery*, 1828, 1835
Soyer, Alexis *The Modern Housewife*, 1849
Street, W M, *The Frugal Housewife*, 1811
*The Accomplished Lady's Closet of Rarities, or the Ingenious
Gentlewoman's Delightful Companion*, 1653
Trusler, *Domestic Management*

SOURCES OF ILLUSTRATIONS

Bust of Dr Kitchiner reproduced by kind permission of the British Library; The Gordon Riots, Cartoons:– Ladies Taking Tea, Gentlemen after Dinner, The Kentish Hop Merchant, Martin's Bill in Operation all reproduced by courtesy of the Trustees of the British Museum; The Cook's Oracle, cartoon by Thomas Hood from *Whims and Oddities* by Thomas Hood 1826; Conversazione, The Committee of Taste, cartoons from *Seven Centuries of English Cooking* by Maxime Hendry, published by Weidenfeld and Nicholson; The East Side of Fitzroy Square reproduced by kind permission of the Corporation of London, Guildhall, London; Portrait of Grimod de la Reynière from *Le Memorial de la Patisserie*, Pierre Lacam 1895; Dr Kitchiner with his Telescope, Hulton Picture Library; Dr Kitchiner's Rotary Oven from *The Golden Age of Cookery*, Tom Bridge 1983; Alexis Soyer with his Magic Stove from *The Modern Housewife*, Alexis Soyer 1848; 1st and 2nd Courses from *The English Housekeeper*, Elizabeth Raffald 1769; St Clement Danes Church, drawing by Neil Foster 1827; Title page, The English Grace, Bubble and Squeak all from *The Cook's Oracle*, Dr Kitchiner 1817; Dr Kitchiner's last letter, 1827; Charming Well Again, cartoon, Eric Quayle; Trussing fork, Larding needle, Meat saw, Paste jigger, Trussing needle, Bottle jack, Dutch oven, Hanging gridiron, Fish kettles, Saucepans all from *Warne's Model Cookery*, 1868; Venison, Cod's Head, Beef, Mutton, Sucking Pigs, Woodcock and Snipe, Veal, Eel, Aitch Bone, Calf's Head all from *A New System of Domestic Cookery*, Mrs Rundle 1806; Artichoke, Fruit Pie from *Le Vrai Cuisinier François*, F.P. de la Varenne 1699; Raised Pie from *The Modern Cook* 1896 ed. C.E. Fracatelli; Milking, Churning from *The English Mother's Catechism* 1824; Sowing from *The House that Jack Built* 1820.

INDEX